# PRIMARY MATHEMATICS
### Standards Edition

## TEXTBOOK

Marshall Cavendish Education

Singapore Math Inc®

W9-API-158

1B

Blank

Original edition published under the title Primary Mathematics Textbook 1B
© 1981 Curriculum Planning & Development Division, Ministry of Education, Singapore
Published by Times Media Private Limited

This edition © 2008 Marshall Cavendish International (Singapore) Private Limited
© 2014 Marshall Cavendish Education Pte Ltd
*(Formerly known as Marshall Cavendish International (Singapore) Private Limited)*

**Published by Marshall Cavendish Education**
Times Centre, 1 New Industrial Road, Singapore 536196
Customer Service Hotline: (65) 6213 9444
US Office Tel: (1-914) 332 8888 I Fax: (1-914) 332 8882
E-mail: tmesales@mceducation.com
Website: www.mceducation.com

Marshall Cavendish Corporation
99 White Plains Road
Tarrytown, NY 10591
U.S.A.
Tel: (1-914) 332 8888
Fax: (1-914) 332 8882
E-mail: mcc@marshallcavendish.com
Website: www.marshallcavendish.com

Singapore Math Inc®
Distributed by
**Singapore Math Inc.**®
19535 SW 129th Avenue
Tualatin, OR 97062
U.S.A.
Website: www.singaporemath.com

First published 2008
Reprinted 2008, 2010, 2011 (twice), 2012, 2014, 2015

Marshall Cavendish is a trademark of Times Publishing Limited.

Singapore Math® is a trademark of Singapore Math Inc.® and
Marshall Cavendish Education Pte Ltd.

Primary Mathematics (Standards Edition) Textbook 1B
ISBN 978-0-7614-6976-6

Printed in Malaysia

Primary Mathematics (Standards Edition) is adapted from Primary Mathematics Textbook 1B (3rd Edition), originally
developed by the Ministry of Education, Singapore. This edition contains new content developed by Marshall Cavendish
International (Singapore) Private Limited, which is not attributable to the Ministry of Education, Singapore.

We would like to acknowledge the Project Team from the Ministry of Education, Singapore, that developed the original
Singapore Edition:
Project Director: Dr Kho Tek Hong
Team Members: Hector Chee Kum Hoong, Liang Hin Hoon, Lim Eng Tann,
                Ng Siew Lee, Rosalind Lim Hui Cheng, Ng Hwee Wan

Our thanks to Richard Askey, Emeritus Professor of Mathematics (University of Wisconsin, Madison) and Madge Goldman,
President (Gabriella and Paul Rosenbaum Foundation), for their help and advice in the production of Primary Mathematics
(Standards Edition).

We would also like to recognize the contribution of Jennifer Kempe (Curriculum Advisor, Singapore Math Inc.®) to
Primary Mathematics (Standards Edition).

# PREFACE

**PRIMARY MATHEMATICS** **(Standards Edition)**
is a complete program from the publishers of
Singapore's successful *Primary Mathematics*
series. Newly adapted to align with the
Mathematics Framework for California Public
Schools, the program aims to equip students
with sound concept development, critical
thinking and efficient problem-solving skills.

**Mathematical concepts** are introduced in the
opening pages and taught to mastery through
specific learning tasks that allow for immediate
assessment and consolidation.

The **Concrete → Pictorial → Abstract**
approach enables students to encounter math
in a meaningful way and translate mathematical
skills from the concrete to the abstract.

The **pencil icon** Exercise 8, page 88 provides
quick and easy reference from the Textbook
to the relevant Workbook pages. The **direct
correlation** of the Workbook to the Textbook
facilitates focused review and evaluation.

The color patch    is
used to invite active student
participation and to facilitate
lively discussion about the
mathematical concepts taught.

New mathematical concepts are introduced through a **spiral progression** that builds on concepts already taught and mastered.

## MULTIPLICATION

**14**

**1** Adding Equal Groups

Count each type of fruit.

$5 + 5 + 5 =$ 

3 fives =

There are 5 pears in each group.

$4 + 4 + 4 + 4 + 4 + 4 =$

6 fours =

There are 4 oranges in each group.

$6 + 6 =$

2 sixes =

There are 6 pineapples in each group.

49

**6** Subtraction Within 100

Subtract 2 from 48.

$48 - 2 =$ 

Count backwards 2 ones from 48:

47, 46

$48 - 2$
$40 \quad 8$

Subtract 2 from 8.

96

**Metacognition** is employed as a strategy for learners to monitor their thinking processes in problem solving. Speech and thought bubbles provide guidance through the thought processes, making even the most challenging problems accessible to students.

## GLOSSARY

| Word | Meaning |
|---|---|
| add | To put together. Example: Add 🍒🍒 and 🍒🍒 to get 🍒🍒🍒🍒. |
| addition sentence | $1 + 2 = 3$   $3 + 1 = 4$ These are examples of **addition sentences**. We write '+' to mean add. |
| altogether | How many apples do we have **altogether**? We have 3 apples **altogether**. |

108

The **glossary** effectively combines pictorial representation with simple mathematical definitions to provide a comprehensive reference guide for students.

# CONTENTS

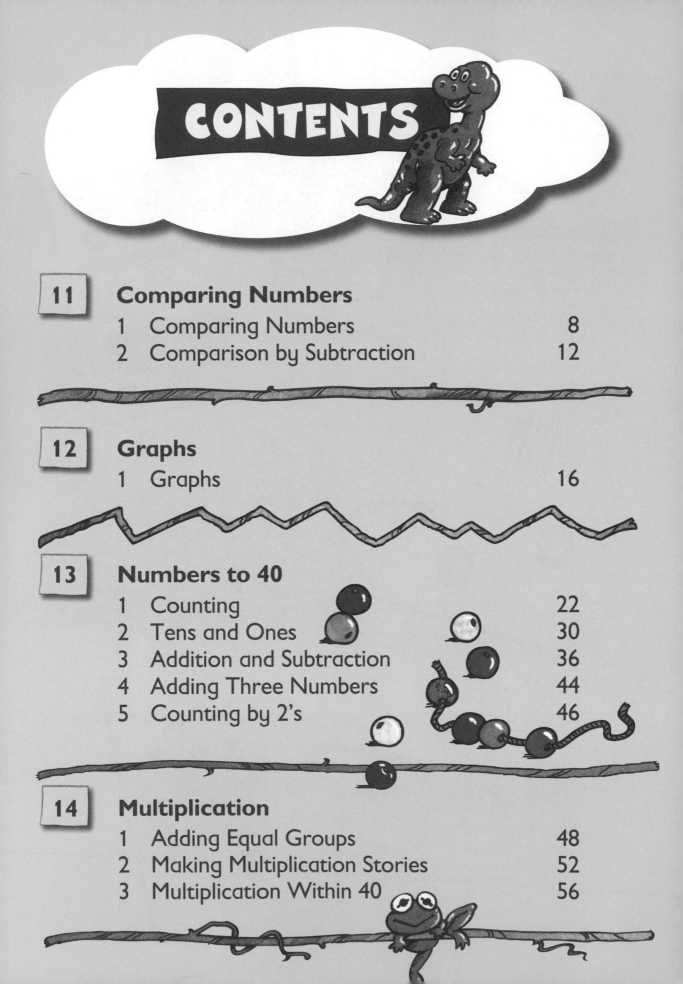

# COMPARING NUMBERS

## 1 Comparing Numbers

Who has more stamps, Matthew or John?

1. Are there more frogs than penguins?

2. Are there more carrots than rabbits?

3. Are there more mangoes than pineapples?

Exercise 1, pages 7-8

4. (a) Which set has more stamps?

3

4

(b) What number is 1 **more** than 3?

5.

What number is 1 more than 8?

6. (a) What number is 1 more than 5?

(b) What number is 1 more than 6?

7. (a) What number is 1 **less** than 7?

(b) What number is 1 less than 6?

8.

What number is 1 less than 10?

9. (a) What number is 1 more than 7?

(b) What number is 1 less than 9?

Exercise 2, pages 9-10

# ② Comparison by Subtraction

There are 3 more flowers than butterflies.
There are 3 fewer butterflies than flowers.

We can compare two numbers by subtraction.

$5 - 2 = 3$

1. Write a number sentence for each story.

(a)

There are 2 more rabbits than carrots.

(b)

Peter                    Juan

Juan has 2 fewer robots than Peter.

(c)

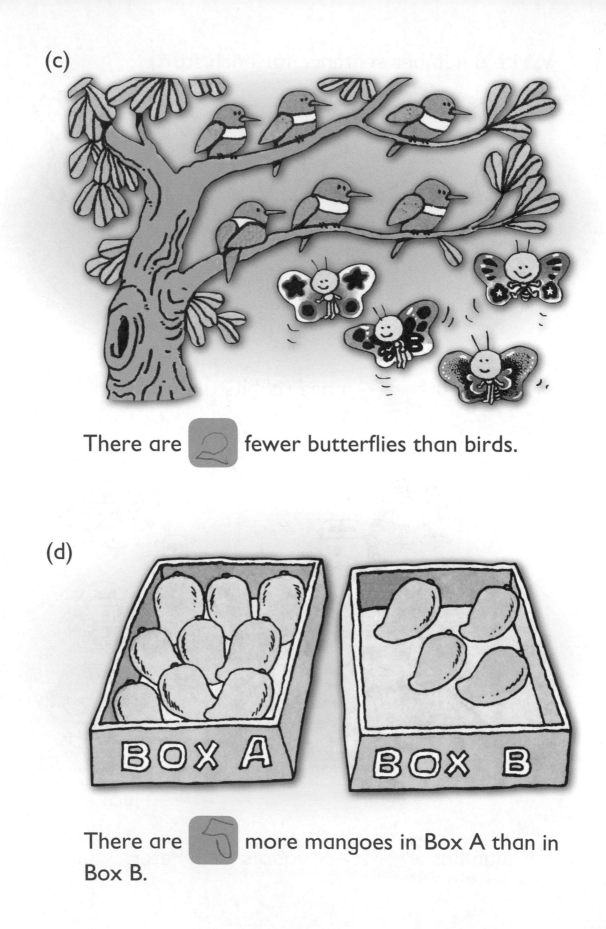

There are 2 fewer butterflies than birds.

(d)

There are 5 more mangoes in Box A than in Box B.

(e)

Amy

Amy has ⟨4⟩ more dolls than robots.

(f)

Sam

Sam buys ⟨5⟩ fewer pineapples than mangoes.

15

Exercises 3 to 6, pages 11-18

## 1 Graphs

Place a color chip on each toy.

Use the same color for each type of toy.

Then make a picture graph like this:

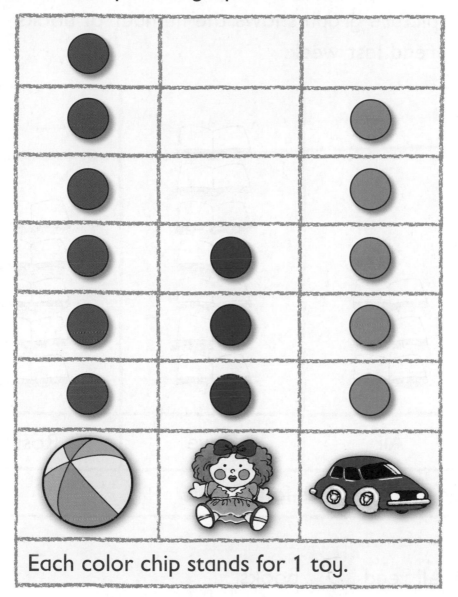

Each color chip stands for 1 toy.

The picture graph shows the number of each type of toy.

How many balls are there?

How many more cars than dolls are there?

How many fewer cars than balls are there?

How many toys are there altogether?

1.  Ali, Dave and Rosni like to read books.
    This picture graph shows the number of books
    they read last week.

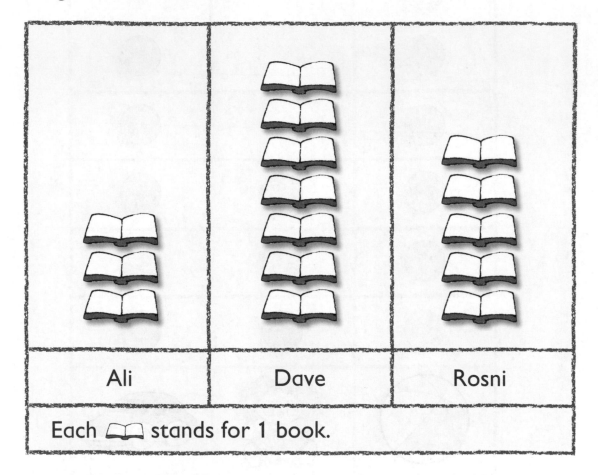

Each 📖 stands for 1 book.

(a) Ali read  3  books.

(b)  Dave  read the most books.

(c) Rosni read  2  more books than Ali.

(d) They read  15  books altogether.

18

Exercises 1 and 2, pages 19-25

2. How many of each fruit are there? Make a tally chart and mark each fruit as you tally.

3. Then, make a bar graph like this.

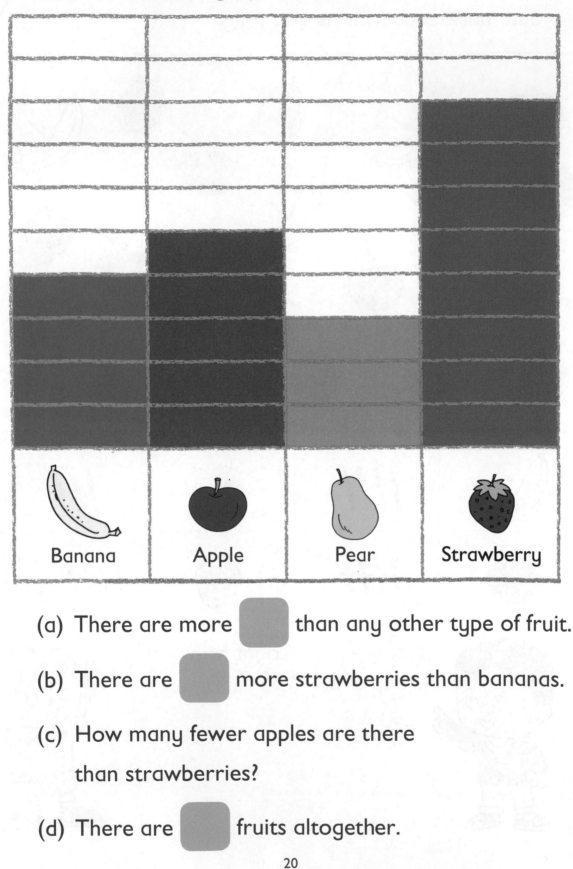

(a) There are more  than any other type of fruit.

(b) There are  more strawberries than bananas.

(c) How many fewer apples are there than strawberries?

(d) There are  fruits altogether.

4. Some children make a tally chart about their favorite ice-cream flavor.

| Flavor | Tally | Number |
|--------|-------|--------|
| Chocolate | 卌 卌 | |
| Vanilla | 卌 ‖ | |
| Strawberry | ‖‖ | |

(a) How many children chose chocolate?

(b) How many children are there altogether?

Then, they make a bar graph like this.

| Chocolate | | | | | | | | | | |
|-----------|--|--|--|--|--|--|--|--|--|--|
| Vanilla | | | | | | | | | | |
| Strawberry | | | | | | | | | | |

(c) Most children chose [ ].

(d) [ ] is the least favorite flavor.

(e) Seven children chose [ ] ice-cream.

(f) How many more children chose chocolate than vanilla?

Exercise 3, pages 26-29

## 13 NUMBERS TO 40

### 1 Counting

Count the beads.

1, 2, 3, 4, 5, 6, 7, 8, 9, 10, 11, 12, 13, 14, 15, 16, 17, 18, 19, 20, . . .

There are more than 20 beads.

# Make tens and count.

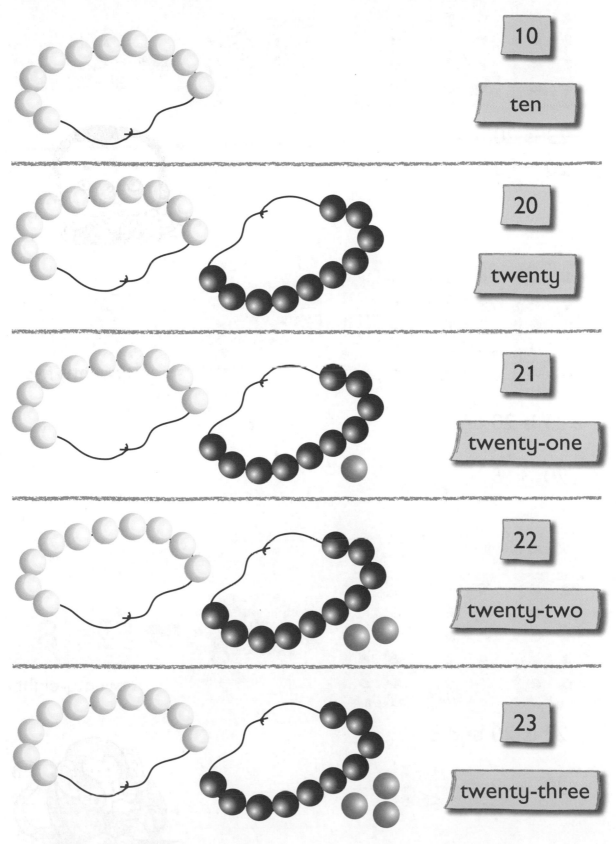

10

ten

20

twenty

21

twenty-one

22

twenty-two

23

twenty-three

23

23 is 20 and 3.

20 + 3 = 23

**1.**

25 is 20 and 5.

20 + 5 = 25

twenty-five

**2.**

28 is 20 and 8.

20 + 8 = 28

twenty-eight

| 1 | 2 | 3 | 4 | 5 | 6 | 7 | 8 | 9 | 10 |
| 11 | 12 | 13 | 14 | 15 | 16 | 17 | 18 | 19 | 20 |
| 21 | 22 | 23 | 24 | 25 | 26 | 27 | 28 | 29 | 30 |
| 31 | 32 | 33 | 34 | 35 | 36 | 37 | 38 | 39 | 40 |

3.

29 and 1 make 30.

29 + 1 = 30

10, 20, 30

3 0

thirty

4.

30 and 4 make 34.

30 + 4 = 34

3 0    4  →  3 4

thirty-four

25

**5.**

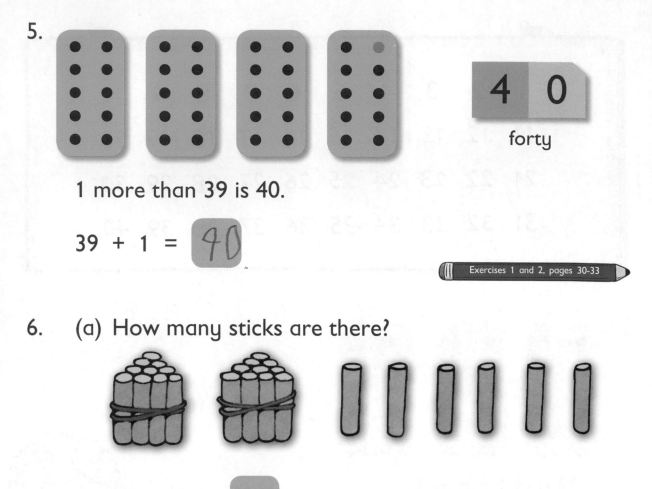

**4 0**

forty

1 more than **39** is **40**.

**39** + **1** = **40**

Exercises 1 and 2, pages 30-33

**6.** (a) How many sticks are there?

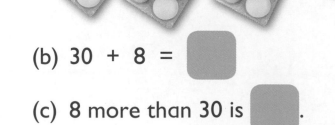

(b) **20** + **6** = ☐

(c) **6** more than **20** is ☐.

**7.** (a) How many eggs are there?

(b) **30** + **8** = ☐

(c) **8** more than **30** is ☐.

Exercise 3, page 34

8.  (a)

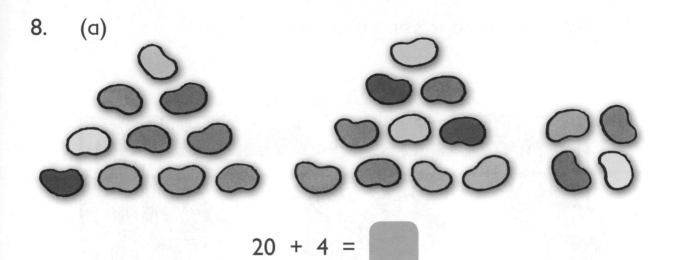

20 + 4 = [ ]

(b)

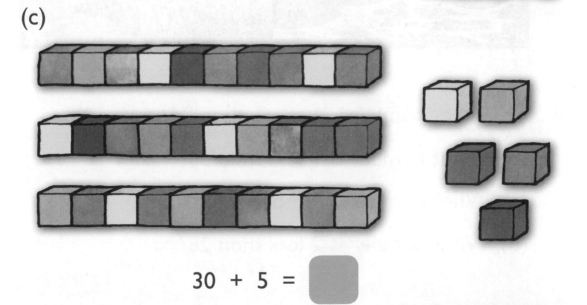

20 + 7 = [ ]

(c)

30 + 5 = [ ]

27

Exercise 4, pages 35-36

9. What are the missing numbers?

10. (a) What number is 1 more than 24?

    (b) What number is 1 less than 30?

    (c) What number is 2 more than 36?

    (d) What number is 2 less than 28?

Exercise 5, pages 37-38

$34 - 27 = \underline{7}$

11. (a) Which is greater, 24 or 27?

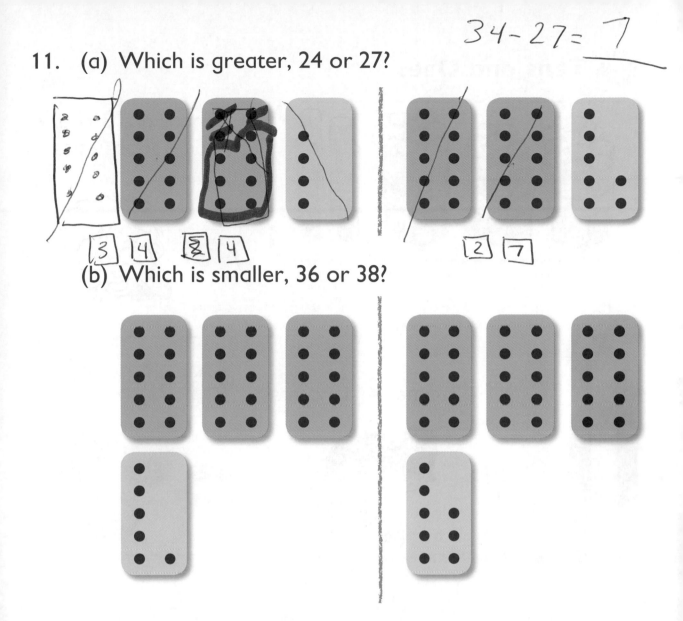

3 4    8 4          2 7

(b) Which is smaller, 36 or 38?

12. Compare these numbers.

34    14    37    24

(a) Which number is the greatest?    1 4

(b) Which number is the smallest?    2 4

(c) Arrange the numbers in order.
    Begin with the smallest.    3 4

    3 7

Exercise 6, page 39

## ② Tens and Ones

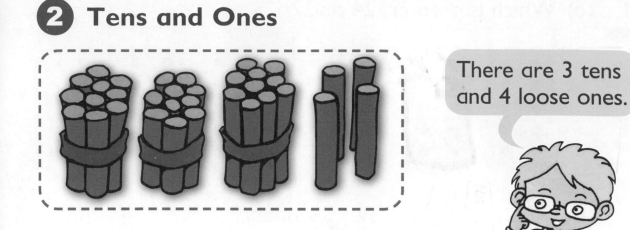

There are 3 tens and 4 loose ones.

1 dime = 10 cents

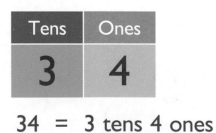

| Tens | Ones |
|------|------|
| 3 | 4 |

34 = 3 tens 4 ones

thirty-four

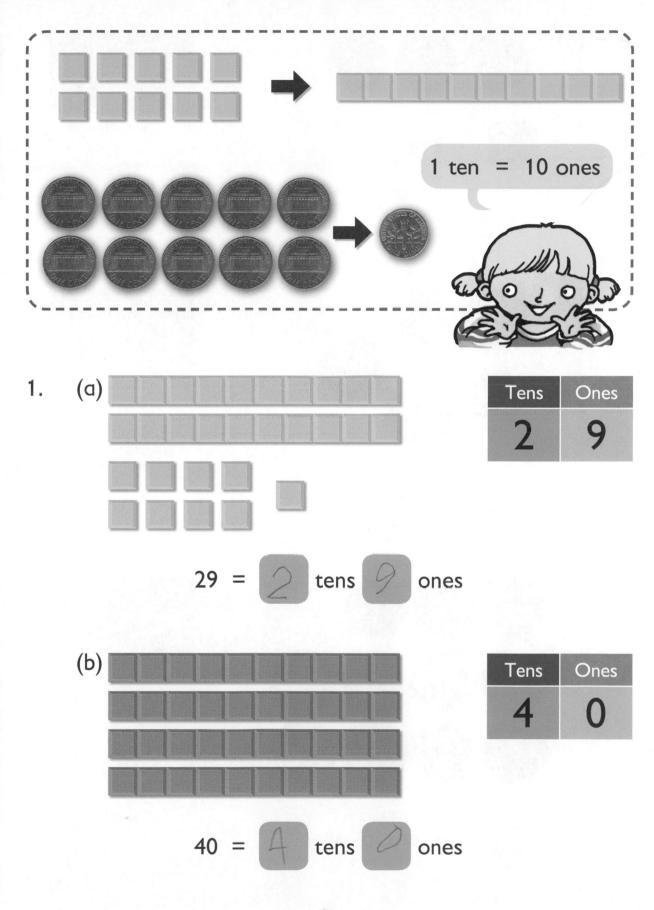

1 ten = 10 ones

1. (a)

| Tens | Ones |
|------|------|
| 2 | 9 |

29 = 2 tens 9 ones

(b)

| Tens | Ones |
|------|------|
| 4 | 0 |

40 = 4 tens 0 ones

2.  (a)

| Tens | Ones |
|------|------|
| 3 | 0 |

 = 3 tens

(b)

| Tens | Ones |
|------|------|
| 2 | 3 |

= 2 tens  3  ones

(c)

| Tens | Ones |
|------|------|
| 3 | 8 |

= 3 tens  8  ones

3.　(a)

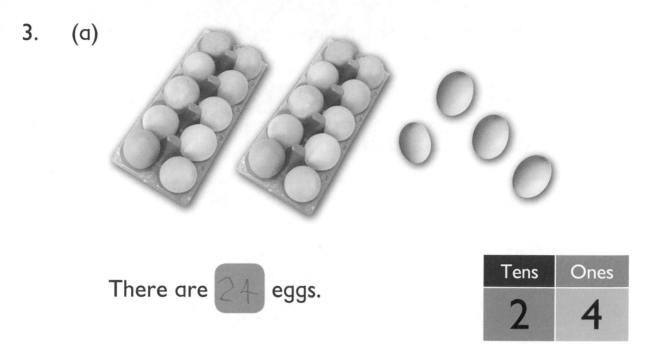

There are ⟨24⟩ eggs.

| Tens | Ones |
|------|------|
| 2 | 4 |

(b)

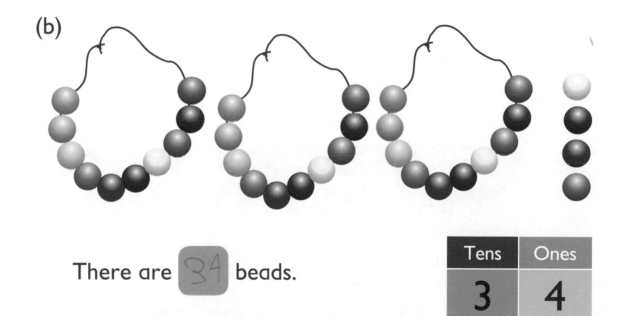

There are ⟨34⟩ beads.

| Tens | Ones |
|------|------|
| 3 | 4 |

(c) Are there more eggs or more ⟨beads?⟩
　　How many more?

33

Exercise 7, pages 40-41

4. (a) What number is 1 more than 24?

(b) What number is 10 more than 24?

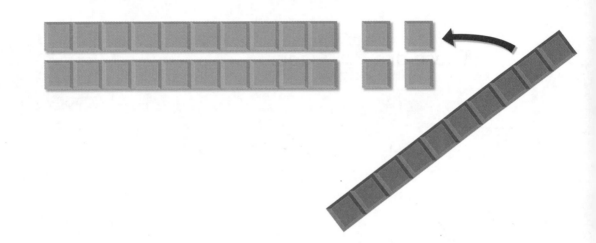

(c) What number is 1 less than 24?

(d) What number is 10 less than 24?

5. (a) What number is 1 more than 29?

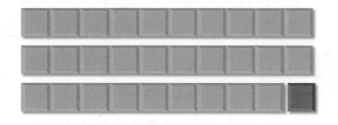

(b) What number is 1 less than 40?

(c) What number is 10 more than 30?

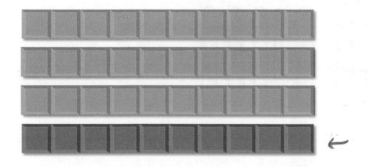

(d) What number is 10 less than 30?

Exercise 8, pages 42-44

# 3 Addition and Subtraction

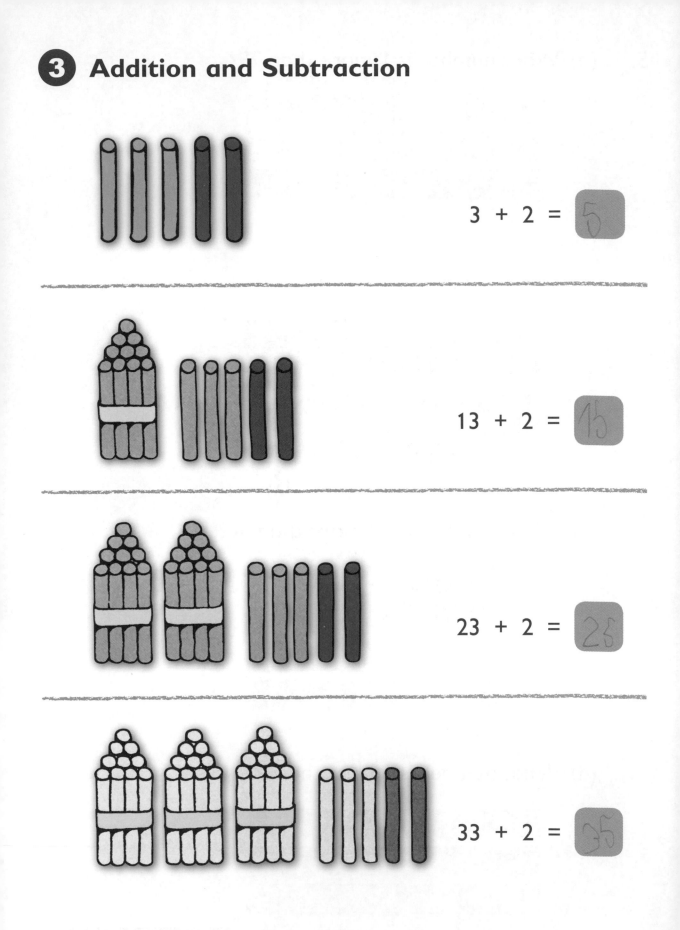

$3 + 2 =$ 5

$13 + 2 =$ 15

$23 + 2 =$ 25

$33 + 2 =$ 35

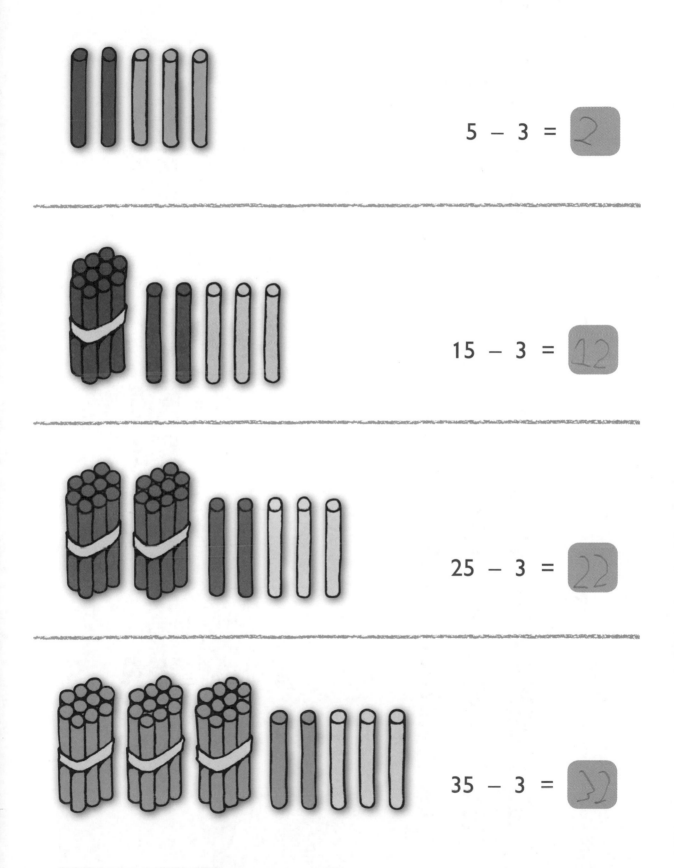

$5 - 3 = 2$

$15 - 3 = 12$

$25 - 3 = 22$

$35 - 3 = 32$

1.  Add or subtract.

(a)

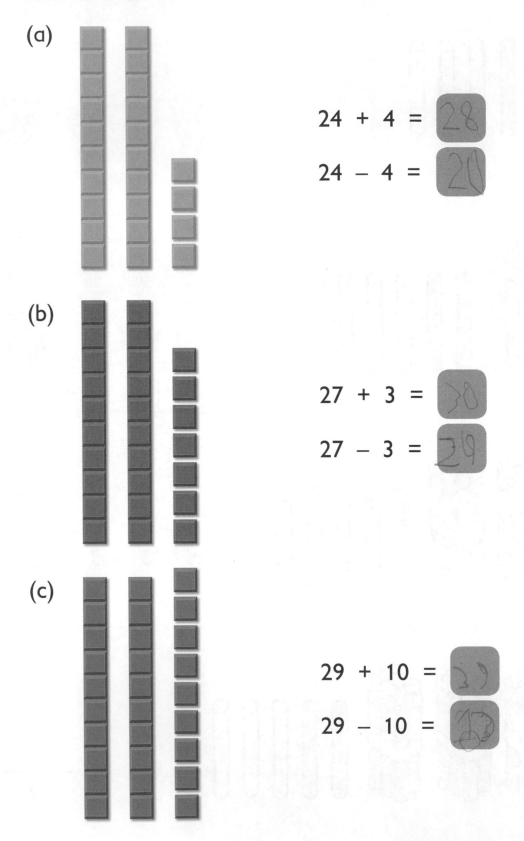

24 + 4 = 28

24 − 4 = 20

(b)

27 + 3 = 30

27 − 3 = 24

(c)

29 + 10 = 39

29 − 10 = 19

Exercises 9 and 10, pages 45-48

2. Add 29 and 3.

27  28  29  30  31  32  33  34  35

Count on from 29: ③⓪, ③①, ③②

29 + 3 = 32

3. Subtract 2 from 31.

26  27  28  29  30  31  32  33  34

Count backwards
from 31: ③⓪, ②⑨

31 – 2 = 29

29

Exercise 11, pages 49-50

4. (a)

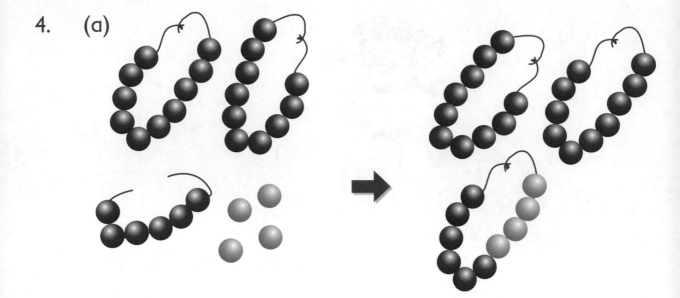

26 + 4 = [ ]     6 + 4 = 10

(b)

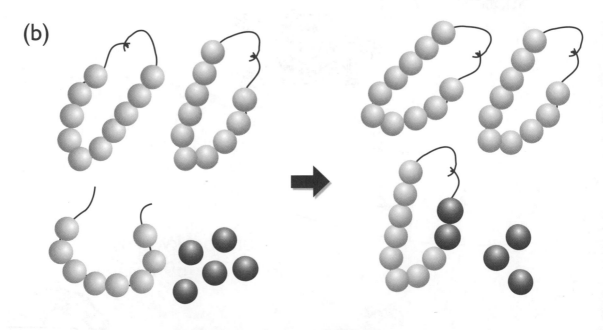

28 + 5 = 33

40

5. (a)

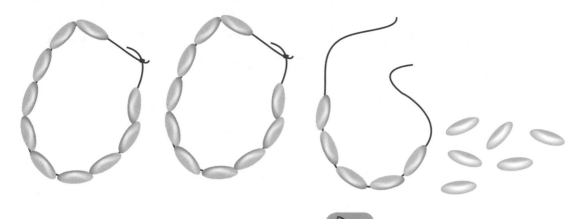

25 + 6 = 31

(b)

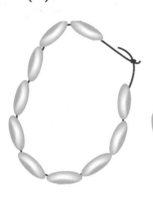
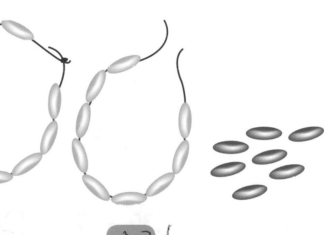

29 + 7 = 37 6

(c)

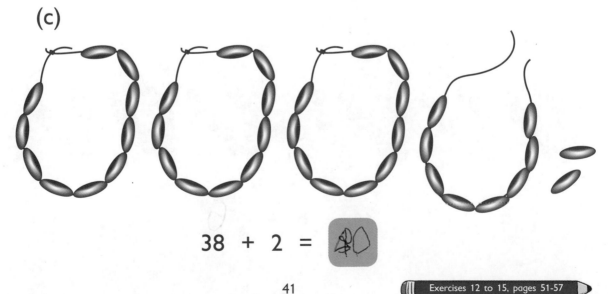

38 + 2 = 40

41

Exercises 12 to 15, pages 51-57

6.  (a)

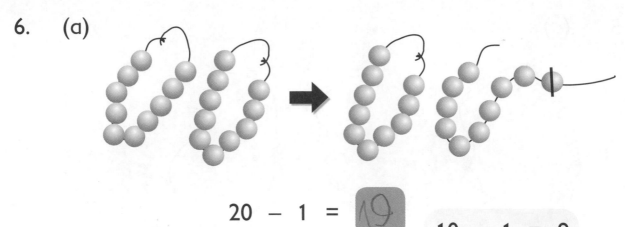

$$20 - 1 = \boxed{19}$$

$$10 - 1 = 9$$

(b)

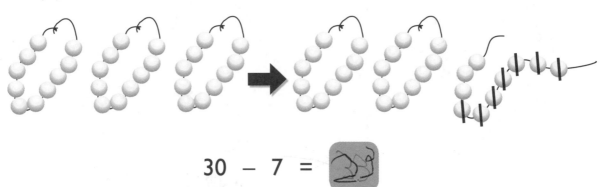

$$30 - 7 = \boxed{23}$$

(c)

$$34 - 8 = \boxed{26}$$

42

**7.** **(a)**

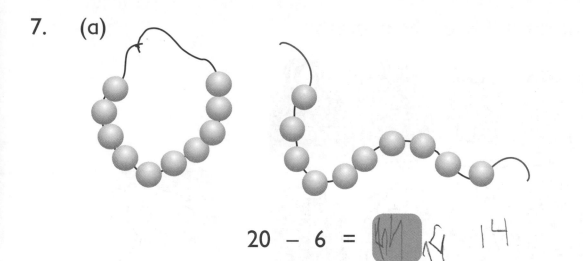

$$20 - 6 = \boxed{14} \quad 14$$

**(b)**

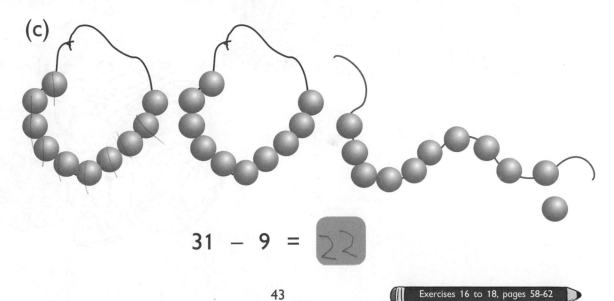

$$30 - 8 = \boxed{22} \quad 22$$

**(c)**

$$31 - 9 = \boxed{22}$$

Exercises 16 to 18, pages 58-62

# 4 Adding Three Numbers

$8 + 2 =$

$8 + 2 + 4 =$

1. (a)

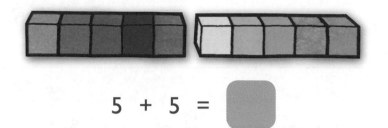

$5 + 5 =$ ☐

(b)

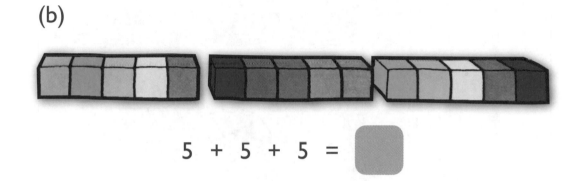

$5 + 5 + 5 =$ ☐

2. Complete the addition sentences.

(a) $4 + 4 + 4 =$ ☐

(b) $6 + 4 + 3 =$ ☐

(c) $3 + 2 + 9 =$ ☐

(d) $6 + 6 + 6 =$ ☐

(e) $7 + 5 + 4 =$ ☐

(f) $8 + 6 + 2 =$ ☐

(g) $8 + 7 + 3 =$ ☐

(h) $8 + 8 + 8 =$ ☐

Exercise 19, pages 63-65

# ⑤ Counting by 2's

We can count by 2's like this:

2, 4, 6, 8, 10

1. Add 2's.

(a) 2 + 2 = 

(b) 2 + 2 + 2 = 

(c) 2 + 2 + 2 + 2 = 

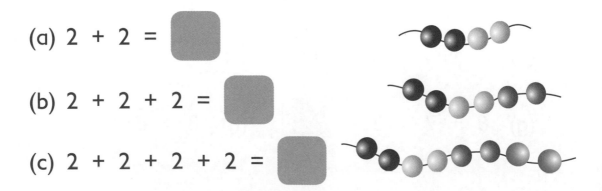

2. Count by 2's.

2, 4, 6, 8, 10, 12, 14, 16, 18, 20

6, 8, 10, ☐ , ☐ , 16, ☐ , ☐ , 22, 24, 26, ☐ , ☐

3. (a) Count backwards by 2's.

Count back by 2's from 18: ⑱, ⑯, ⑭, ⑫

11  12  13  14  15  16  17  18

(b)

16  18  20  22  ☐  ☐  28  ☐  32  ☐  36

Exercise 20, pages 66-67

Review 8, pages 68-73

# 14 MULTIPLICATION

## 1 Adding Equal Groups

Count each type of fruit.

5 + 5 + 5 = ☐

3 fives = ☐

There are 5 pears in each group.

4 + 4 + 4 + 4 + 4 + 4 = ☐

6 fours = ☐

There are 4 oranges in each group.

6 + 6 = ☐

2 sixes = ☐

There are 6 pineapples in each group.

**1.**

There are [ ] rabbits in each group.

There are [ ] rabbits altogether.

**2.**

There are [ ] shells in each group.

There are [ ] shells altogether.

**3.**

There are [ ] boats in each group.

There are [ ] boats altogether.

Exercises 1 and 2, pages 74-77

4.

There are ☐ groups of 3.

There are ☐ carrots altogether.

5.

There are ☐ groups of 4.

There are ☐ cakes altogether.

6.

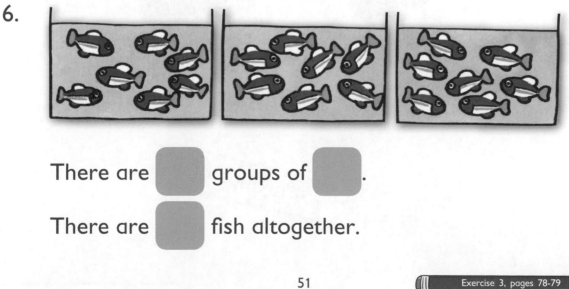

There are ☐ groups of ☐.

There are ☐ fish altogether.

Exercise 3, pages 78-79

# 2 Making Multiplication Stories

2 + 2 + 2 + 2

4 × 2

4 twos

4 groups of 2

5 × 10 = 10 × 5

This is **multiplication**.
It means **putting together
equal groups**.

We write the number sentence:

4 × 2 = 8

2+2+2+2

**Multiply** 4 and 2.
The answer is 8.

There are 4 equal groups.
There are 2 apples in each group.
There are 8 apples altogether.

1. Make up a story for each number sentence.

(a)

$$4 \times 3 = 12$$

There are 4 vases.
There are 3 flowers
in each vase.
There are 12 flowers
altogether.

(b)

$$4 \times 5 = 20$$

(c)

$$4 \times 8 = 32$$

2. Make up a story for each number sentence.

(a)

6+6+6+6    4 × 6 = 24

(b)

6 × 4 = 24

# 3 Multiplication Within 40

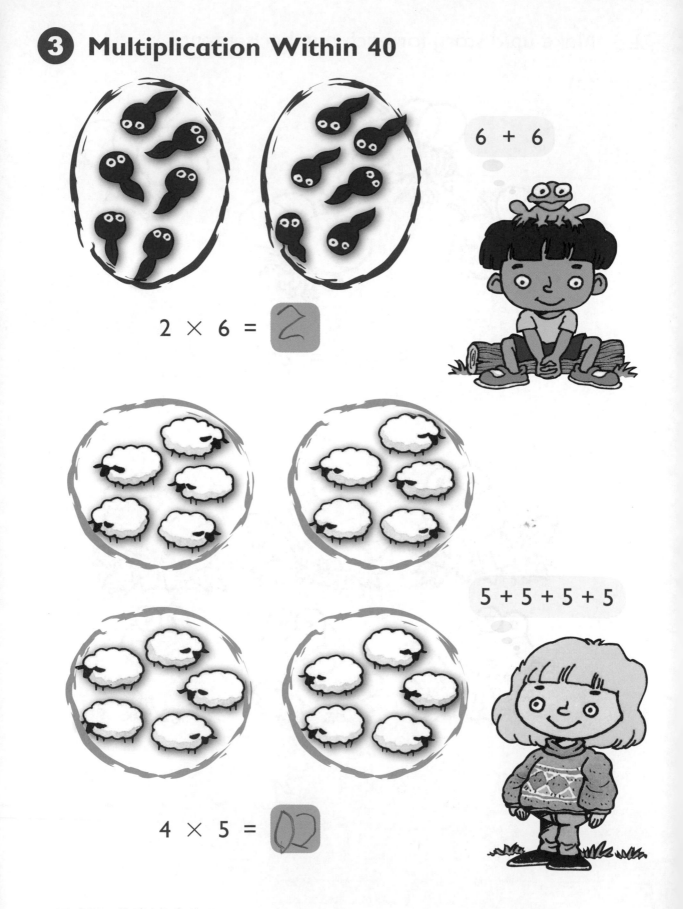

6 + 6

2 × 6 = 2

5 + 5 + 5 + 5

4 × 5 = 02

56

**1.**

How many pears are there altogether?

$$3 \times 2 = 6$$

There are 6 pears altogether.

**2.**

How many sticks are there altogether?

$$4 \times 5 = 20$$

There are 20 sticks altogether.

3. Complete the number sentences.

(a)

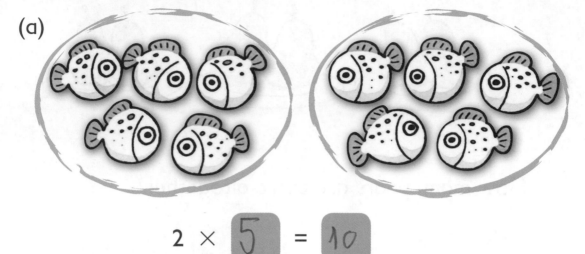

2 × 5 = 10

(b)

5 × 2 = 10

(c)

6 × 3 = 18

Exercise 6, pages 83-85

**4.**

There are 6 stamps in each row.
How many stamps are there in 3 rows?

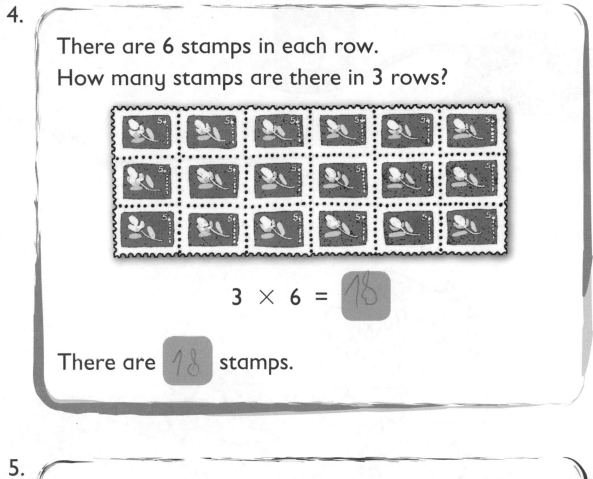

$$3 \times 6 = \boxed{18}$$

There are 18 stamps.

**5.**

Lily made these squares with straws.
How many straws did she use?

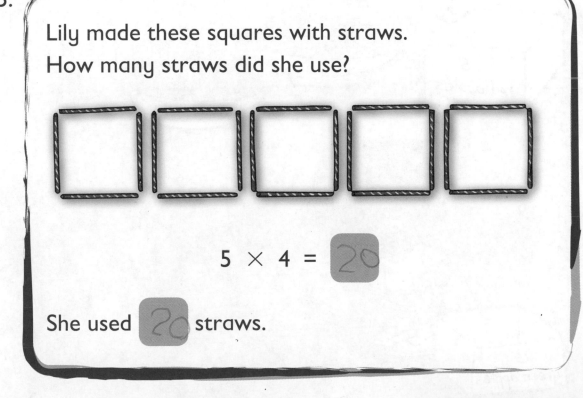

$$5 \times 4 = \boxed{20}$$

She used 20 straws.

Exercise 7, pages 86-88
Reviews 9 to 11, pages 89-100

# 15 DIVISION

## 1 Sharing and Grouping

I put 15 apples equally on 3 plates.

Divide 15 apples into 3 equal groups.

There are ▢ apples in each group.

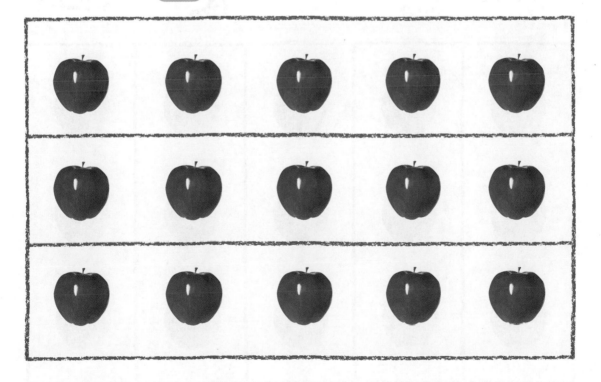

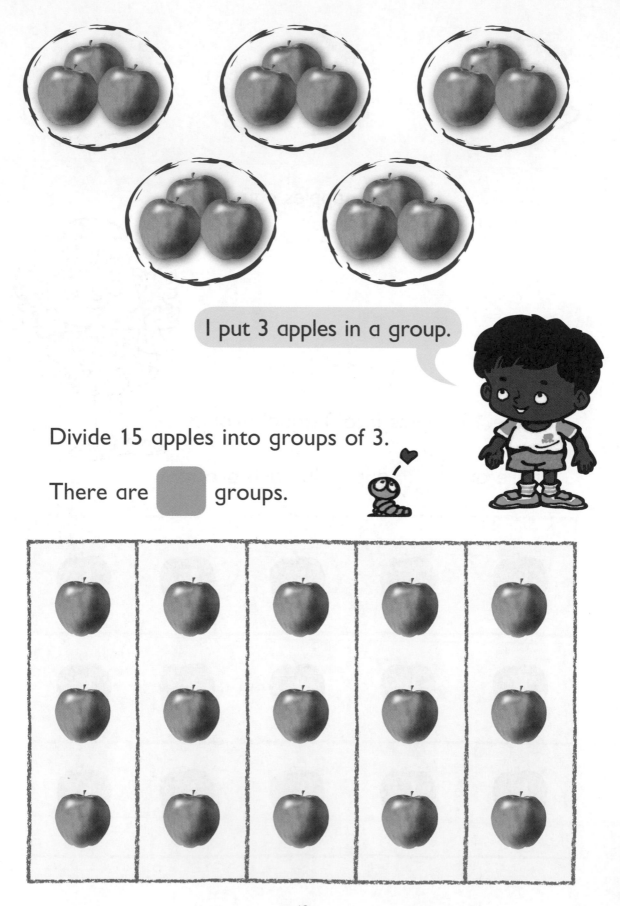

I put 3 apples in a group.

Divide 15 apples into groups of 3.

There are ▢ groups.

1. Divide 10 children into 2 equal groups.
   How many children are there in each group?

There are 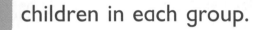 children in each group.

2. Share 12 kiwis equally between 2 children.
   How many kiwis does each child get?

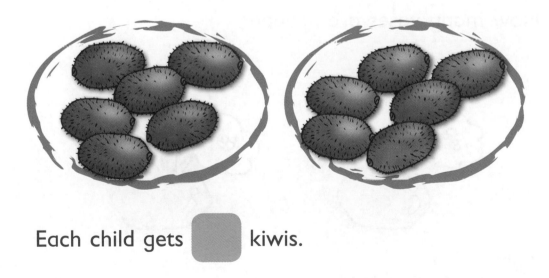

Each child gets ☐ kiwis.

3. Put 14 crayons equally into 2 boxes.
   How many crayons are there in each box?

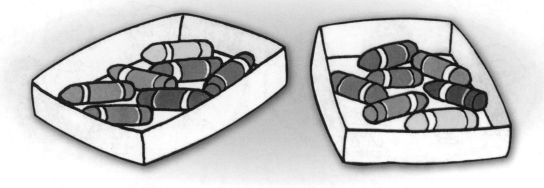

There are [ ] crayons in each box.

Exercises 1 and 2, pages 101-106

4. There are 6 flowers.
   Put 3 flowers in a vase.
   How many vases are needed?

[ ] vases are needed.

5. There are 20 coins.
   Put 5 coins in a group.
   How many groups are there?

There are [ ] groups.

6. Divide 12 mangoes into groups of 3.
   How many groups are there?

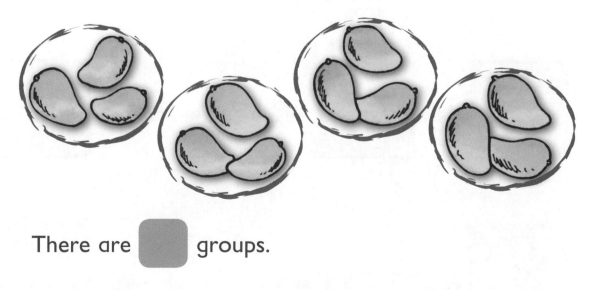

There are [ ] groups.

Exercise 3, pages 107-108

**1** ## Making Halves and Fourths

Fold a piece of square paper into **halves**.

Then fold it into **fourths**.

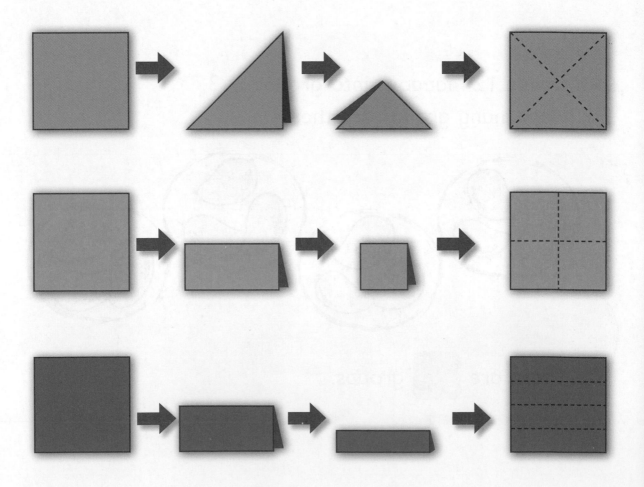

**1.**

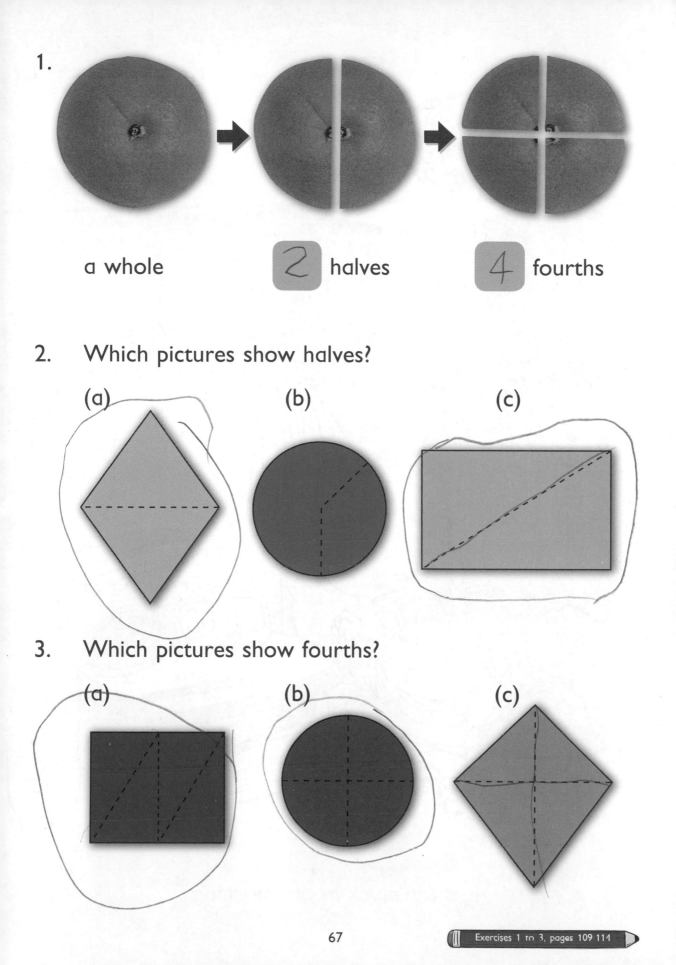

a whole        2 halves        4 fourths

**2.** Which pictures show halves?

(a)        (b)        (c)

**3.** Which pictures show fourths?

(a)        (b)        (c)

Exercises 1 to 3, pages 109 111

# 17 TIME

## 1 Telling Time

It is 6 o'clock in the morning.

1. What time is it?

69

**2.**

| | | |
|---|---|---|
| | **4:00** | It is 4 o'clock. |
| | **4:30** | It is **half past** 4. |
| | **5:00** | It is ___ o'clock. |
| | **7:30** | It is half past ___. |
| | **11:30** | It is half past ___. |

## 3. What time is it?

Exercise 2, pages 118-120

4. Dad gets up after 7 o'clock.

(a) Does he leave for work **after** half past 7?

(b) Does he have breakfast **before** 8:00?

Exercise 3, pages 121-122

## 2 Estimating Time

It is after 9 o'clock.

It is not 10 o'clock yet.

It is close to 10 o'clock.

It is a **little before** 10 o'clock.

It is **about** 10 o'clock.

---

It is after 1 o'clock.

It is not half past 1 yet.

It is **almost** half past 1.

It is about half past 1.

---

It is after 11 o'clock.

It is a **little after** 11 o'clock.

It is about 11 o'clock.

1. Estimate the time.

(a) 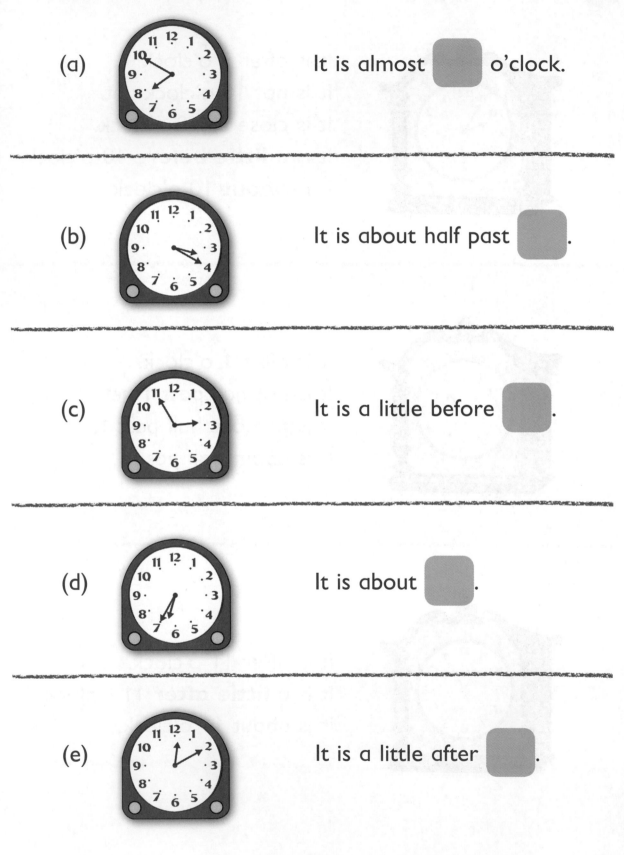 It is almost ⬜ o'clock.

(b) It is about half past ⬜.

(c) It is a little before ⬜.

(d) It is about ⬜.

(e) It is a little after ⬜.

2. Which takes longer?

(a)     or

(b)     or

(c)     or

Exercise 4, pages 123-124

Review 12, pages 125-129

## 1 Tens and Ones

Count by tens.

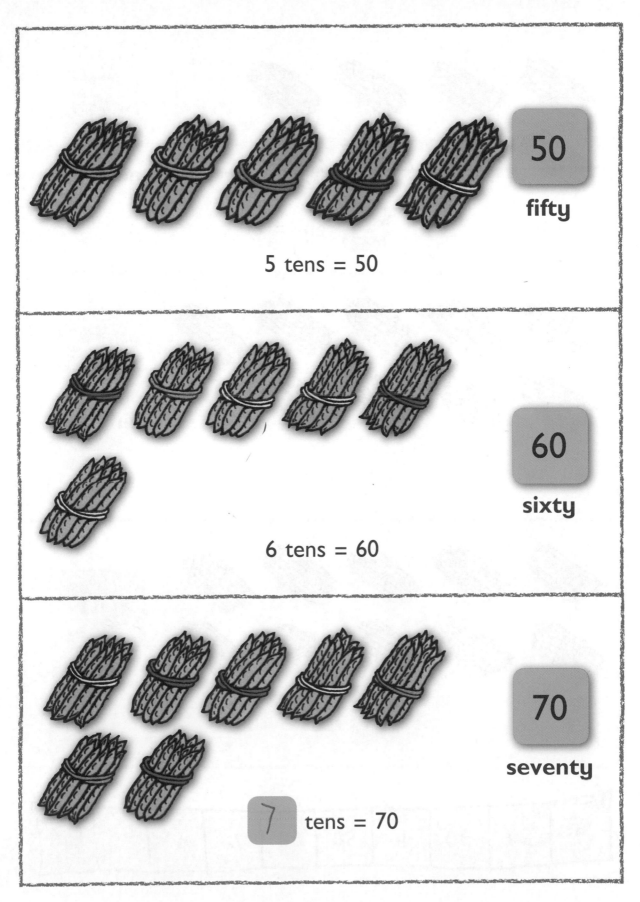

50
**fifty**

5 tens = 50

60
**sixty**

6 tens = 60

70
**seventy**

7 tens = 70

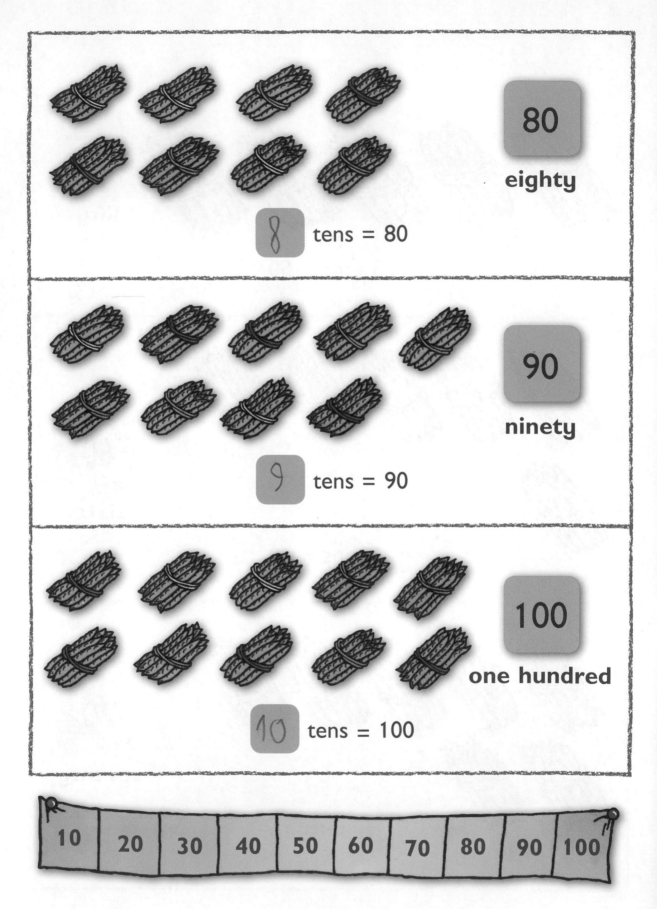

80
**eighty**

8 tens = 80

90
**ninety**

9 tens = 90

100
**one hundred**

10 tens = 100

| 10 | 20 | 30 | 40 | 50 | 60 | 70 | 80 | 90 | 100 |

1.    Count the tens.

(a)

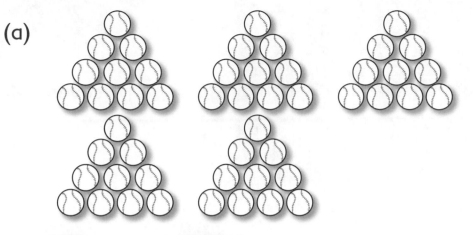

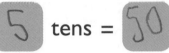

5 tens = 50

(b)

6 tens = 60

(c)

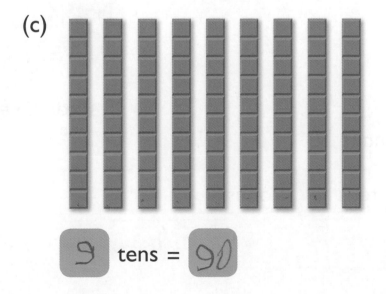

9 tens = 90

Exercise 1, pages 130-132

2. (a)

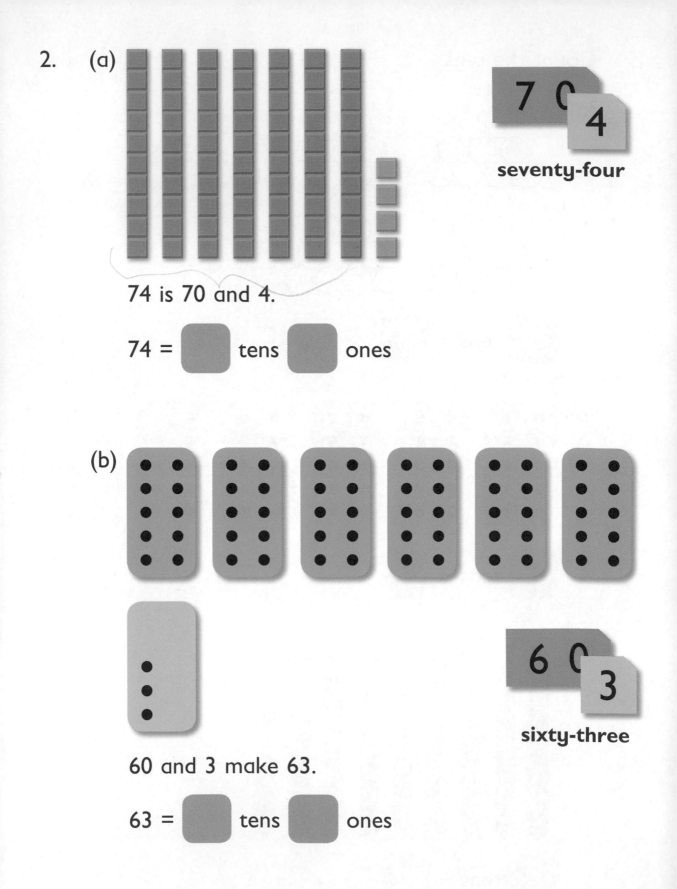

7 0
4

**seventy-four**

74 is 70 and 4.

74 = ☐ tens ☐ ones

(b)

60 and 3 make 63.

6 0
3

**sixty-three**

63 = ☐ tens ☐ ones

80

3. Count the tens and ones.

(a)

5 tens 3 ones = 53

(b)

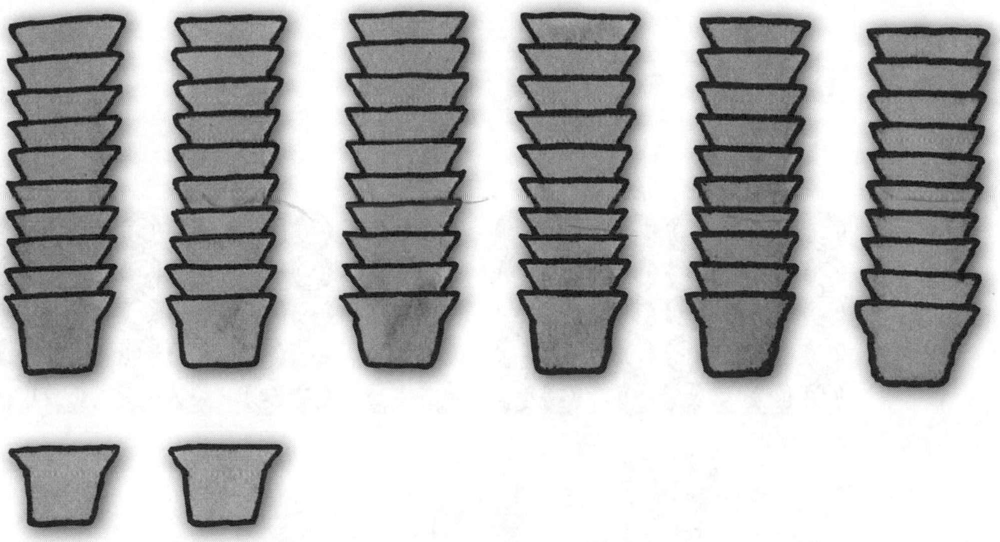

6 tens 2 ones = 62

(c)

4 tens 2 ones = 42

81

Exercises 2 to 4, pages 133-138

4.   (a)

70 + 1 = 71

(b)

70 + 6 = 76   0666

(c)

80 + 8 = 88

82

## 2 Estimation

1.  Diego has 3 similar jars.

    There are about 10 marbles in Jar A.

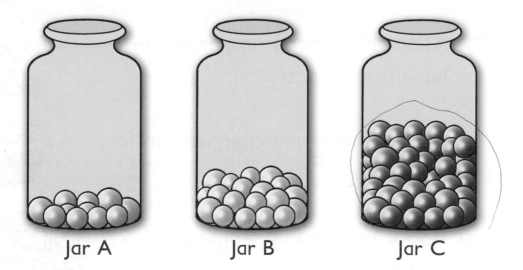

Jar A          Jar B          Jar C

(a) About how many marbles are there in Jar B?

   There are about  15  marbles in Jar B.

(b) About how many marbles are there in Jar C?

   There are about  25  marbles in Jar C.

(c) Diego tries to put the marbles from
   Jars A, B and C in his pockets.

   About how many marbles do you think
   Diego has in his pockets?

   There are about  50  marbles altogether
   in Diego's pockets.

2. Estimate.

(a) About how many marbles can
you hold in your hands? 11

(b) About how many grapes are in a
bunch of grapes? 13

(c) About how many cherries can fit
in this bowl? 30

(d) About how many people can
a bus hold? 5

3.

(a) There are about 50 people at the beach.

(b) There are exactly 19 people at the beach.

Exercise 6, page 141

# 3 Order of Numbers

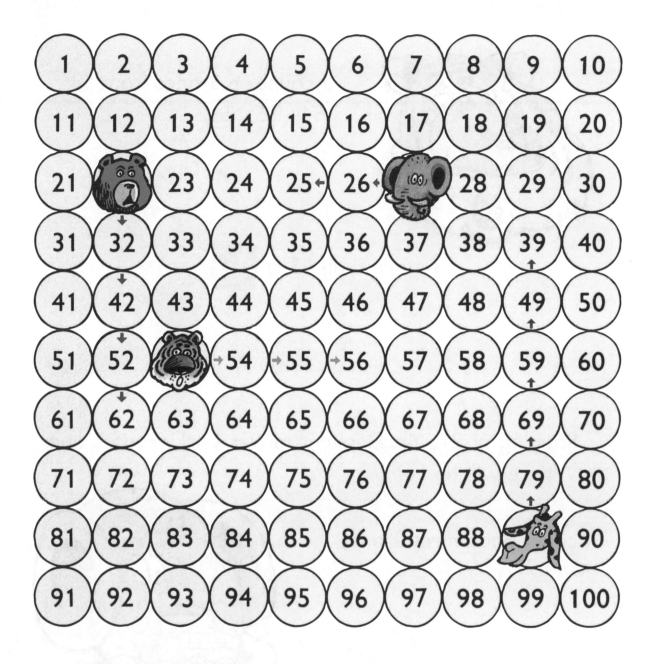

Mr. Tiger is at 53.

Where are Mr. Elephant, Mrs. Bear and Miss Giraffe?

Starting at 53, Mr. Tiger moves on 3 ones.
Where will he be?

I count on 3 ones from 53:
54, 55, 56

3 more than 53 is 56 .

Starting at 27, Mr. Elephant moves backwards 2 ones.
Where will he be?

I count backwards 2 ones
from 27: 26, 25

2 less than 27 is 25 .

Starting at 22, Mrs. Bear moves on 4 tens.
Where will she be?

I count on 4 tens from 22:
(32), (42), (52), (62)

40 more than 22 is  62 .

Starting at 89, Miss Giraffe moves backwards 5 tens.
Where will she be?

I count backwards 5 tens from 89:
(79), (69), (59), (49), (39)

50 less than 89 is 39 .

**1.**

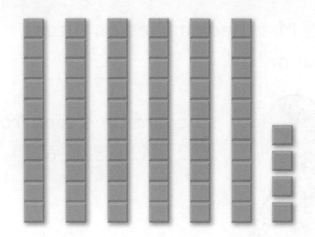

(a) What number is 1 more than 64?

(b) What number is 1 less than 64?

(c) What number is 10 more than 64?

(d) What number is 10 less than 64?

**2.** The numbers below count on or backwards in a regular pattern.

What are the missing numbers?

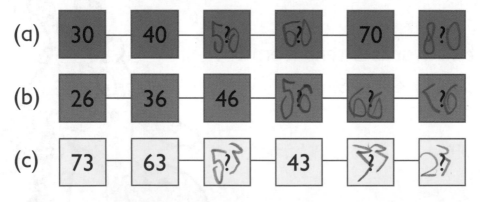

(a) 30 — 40 — 5? — 6? — 70 — 8?0

(b) 26 — 36 — 46 — 5? — 6? — ?6

(c) 73 — 63 — 5?3 — 43 — ?3 — 2?

**3.** (a) What number is 10 more than 52?

(b) What number is 20 more than 52?

(c) What number is 10 less than 96?

(d) What number is 20 less than 96?

Exercises 7 to 12, pages 142-149

# 4 Comparing Numbers

I always take the greater amount.

21 is greater than 12.

We write: **21 > 12**

99 is less than 100.

We write: **99 < 100**

This sign means **greater than**.

This sign means **less than**.

1. Which sign should you use, **>** or **<**?

(a)

43 ⊘ 34

(b)

69 **<** 78

(c) 35 **>** 32          (d) 29 **<** 37

(e) 47 **<** 50          (f) 50 **>** 49

2. (a) Which number is smaller, 40 or 39?

(b) Which number is greater, 29 or 30?

(c) Which number is the smallest, 65, 64 or 56?

(d) Which number is the greatest, 89, 90 or 98?

3. Arrange the numbers in order.
   Begin with the smallest.

59   95   90   50

# **5** Addition Within 100

Add 54 and 3.

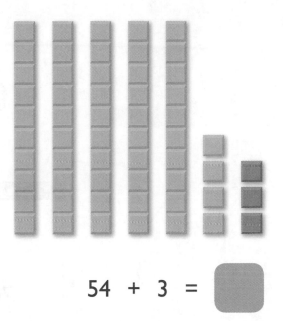

54 + 3 = [ ]

Count on 3 ones from 54:
(55), (56), (57)

54 + 3
/  \
50   4
Add 4 and 3.

1.

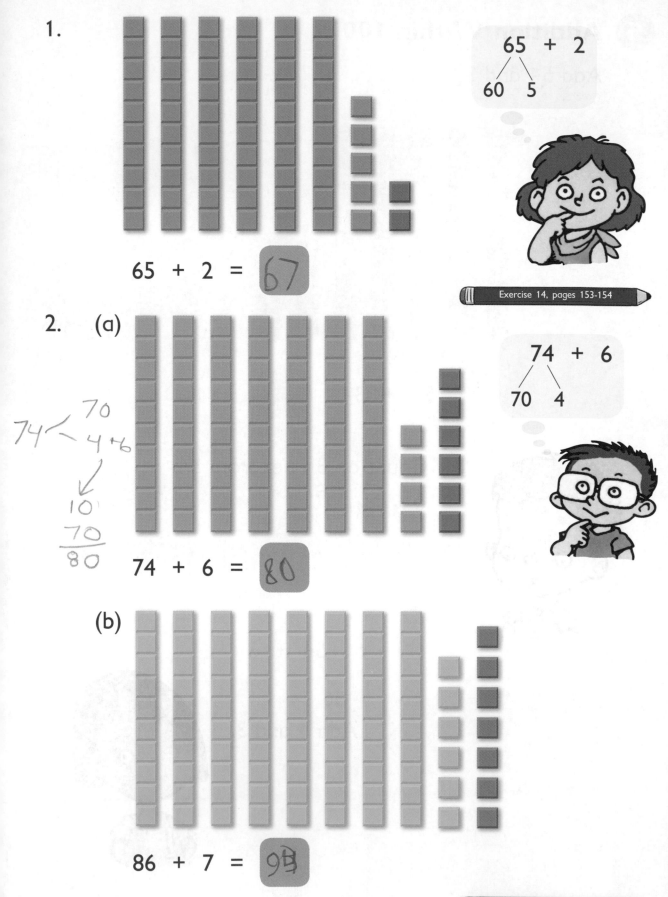

$$65 + 2$$
60   5

$$65 + 2 = 67$$

Exercise 14, pages 153-154

2.   (a)

$$74 + 6$$
70   4

74 < 70
      4 +6
      ↓
     10
     70
     ——
     80

$$74 + 6 = 80$$

(b)

$$86 + 7 = 93$$

92

Exercise 15, pages 155-156

**3.** Add 62 and 30.

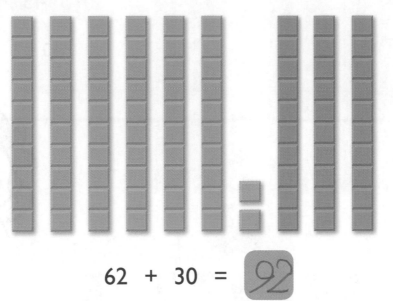

62 + 30 = 92

Count on 3 tens from 62:
72 , 82 , 92

62 + 30
60   2

Add 60 and 30.

4.   (a)

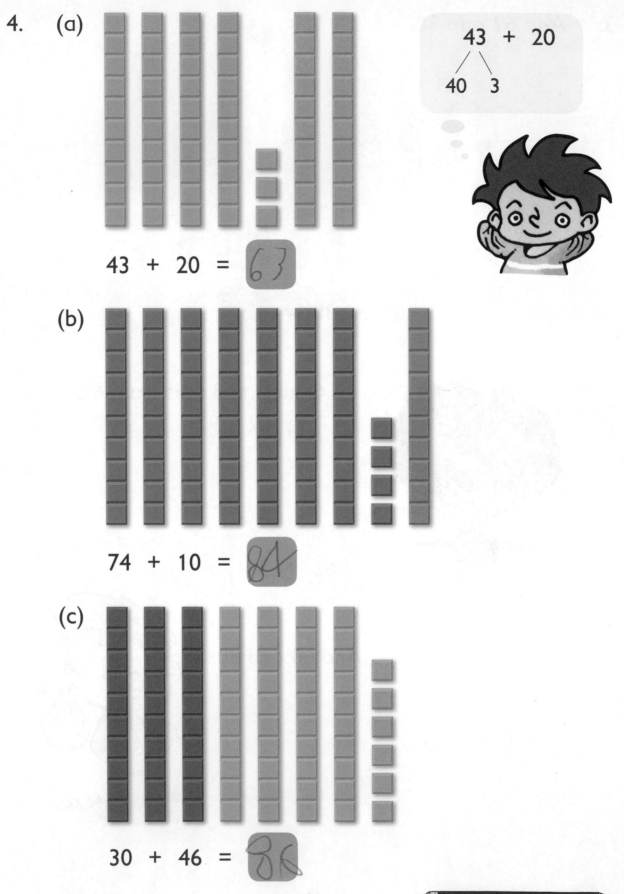

43  +  20

40    3

43  +  20  =  63

(b)

74  +  10  =  84

(c)

30  +  46  =  86

94

Exercises 16 and 17, pages 157-160

5. Add 32 and 16.

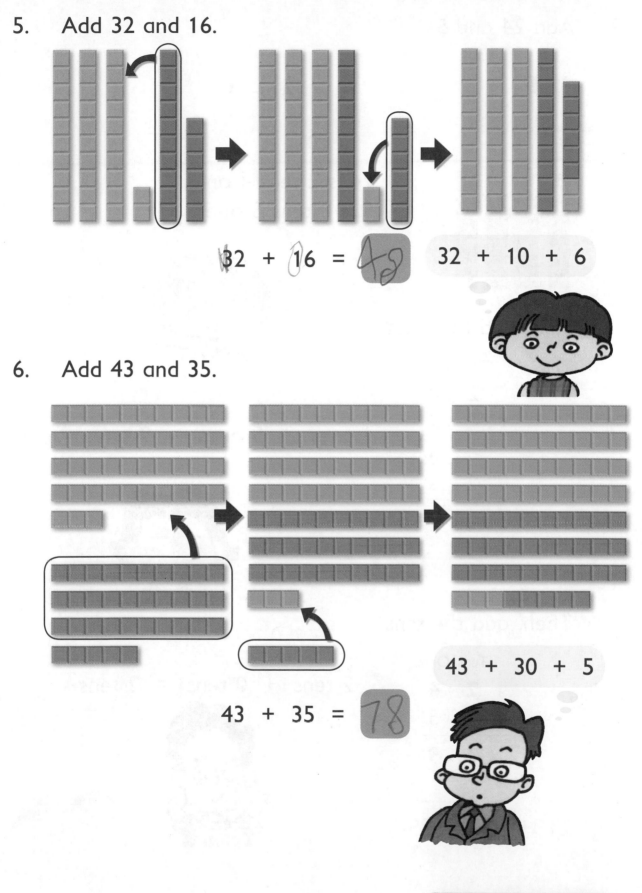

32 + 16 = 48    32 + 10 + 6

6. Add 43 and 35.

43 + 30 + 5

43 + 35 = 78

Exercise 18, pages 161-162

7. Add 24 and 5.

$$24 + 5$$

20    4

24 is 2 tens 4 ones.
5 is 0 tens 5 ones.

First, add the ones.

| Tens | Ones |
|------|------|
| 2 | **4** |
| + | **5** |
| | **9** |

4 ones + 5 ones = 9 ones

Then, add the tens.

| Tens | Ones |
|------|------|
| **2** | 4 |
| + | 5 |
| **2** | 9 |

2 tens + 0 tens = 2 tens

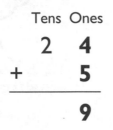

24 + 5 = 29

8.   Add 52 and 6.

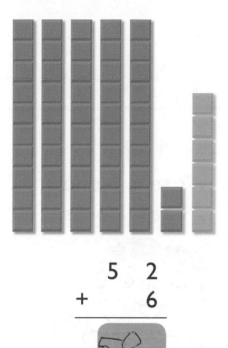

52 + 6
50   2

52 is 5 tens 2 ones.
6 is 0 tens 6 ones.

```
    5   2
+       6
_____
    58
```

9.   Add 71 and 4.

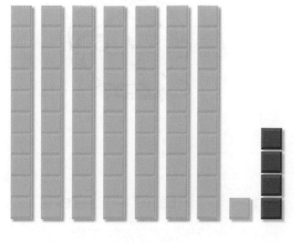

```
    7   1
+       4
_____
    75
```

97

10.  Add 26 and 12.

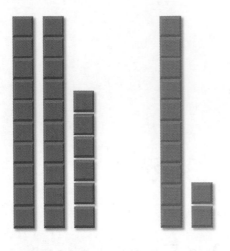

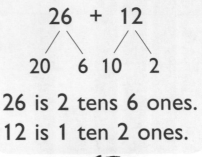

First, add the ones.

Tens Ones

$$
\begin{array}{cc}
 & 2 \ \ 6 \\
+ & 1 \ \ 2 \\
\hline
 & 8
\end{array}
$$

6 ones + 2 ones = 8 ones

Then, add the tens.

Tens Ones

$$
\begin{array}{cc}
 & 2 \ \ 6 \\
+ & 1 \ \ 2 \\
\hline
 & 3 \ \ 8
\end{array}
$$

2 tens + 1 ten = 3 tens

26 + 12 = 38

11. Add 43 and 15.

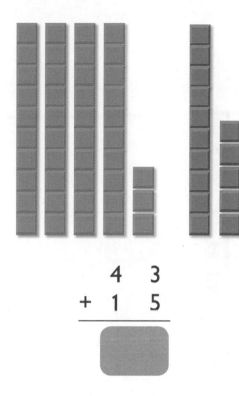

$$43 + 15$$

40   3   10   5

43 is 4 tens 3 ones.
15 is 1 ten 5 ones.

```
    4  3
 +  1  5
 _____
```

12. Add 62 and 27.

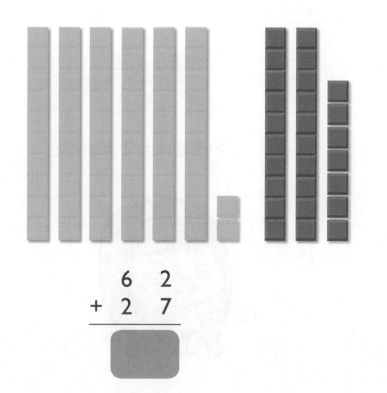

```
    6  2
 +  2  7
 _____
```

Exercises 19, pages 163-166

# **6** Subtraction Within 100

Subtract 2 from 48.

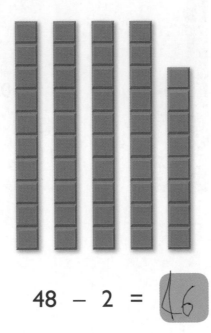

$$48 - 2 = \boxed{46}$$

Count backwards 2 ones from 48:
(47), (46)

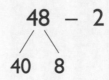

$$48 - 2$$
$$40 \quad 8$$

Subtract 2 from 8.

1. (a)

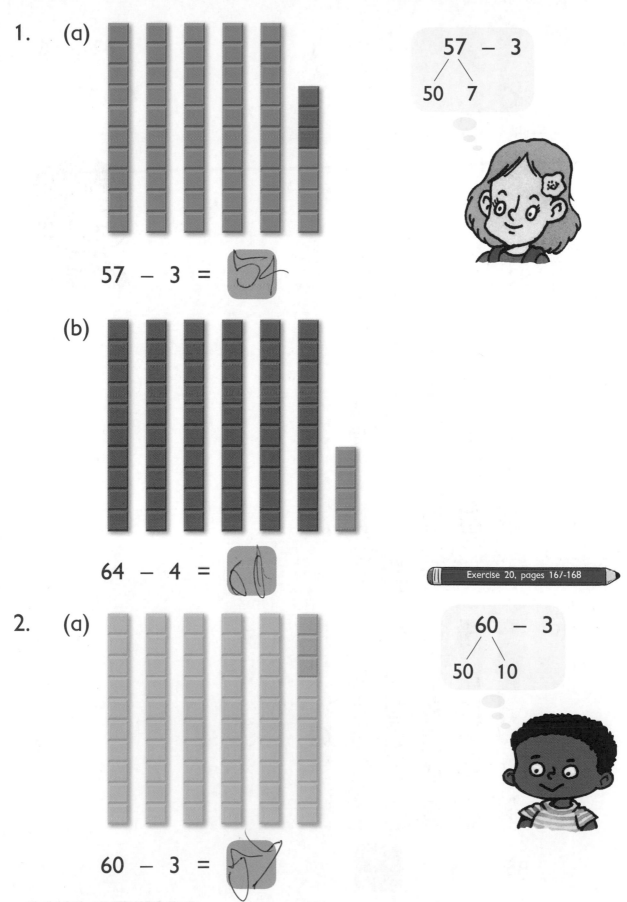

57 − 3 = 54

57 − 3

50   7

(b)

64 − 4 = 60

Exercise 20, pages 167-168

2. (a)

60 − 3 = 57

60 − 3

50   10

101

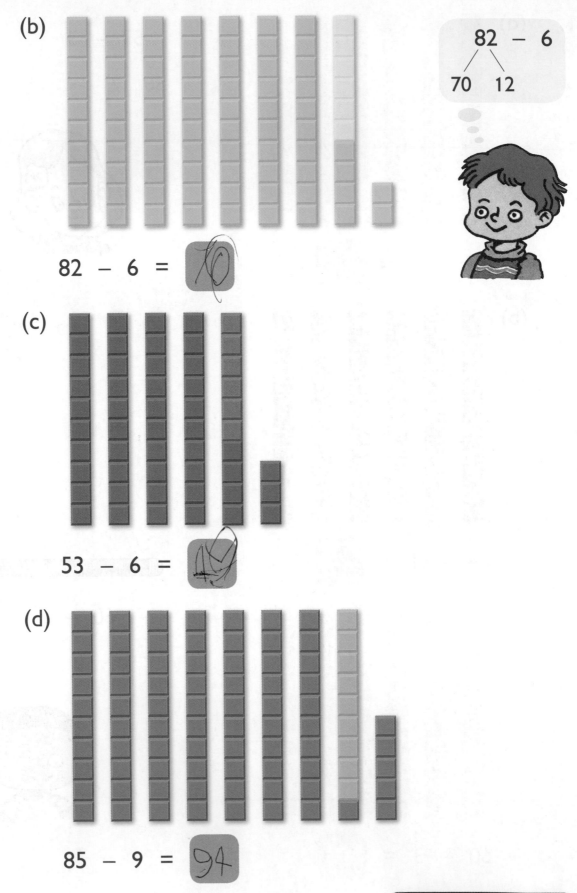

(b)

82 – 6

70    12

82 – 6 =

(c)

53 – 6 =

(d)

85 – 9 = 94

102

Exercise 21, pages 169-170

3. Subtract 20 from 53.

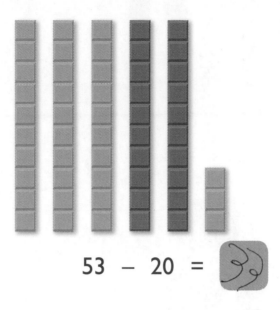

$$53 - 20 = \boxed{33}$$

Count backwards 2 tens from 53:
43, 33

$$53 - 20$$
$$50 \quad 3$$
Subtract 20 from 50.

4. (a)

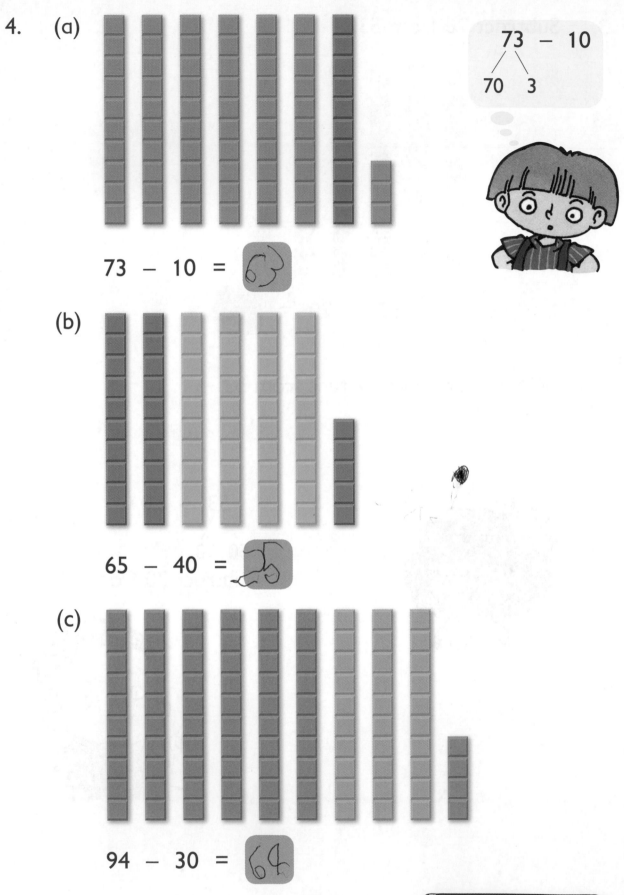

$$73 - 10$$
$$\diagup \quad \diagdown$$
$$70 \quad 3$$

73 − 10 = 63

(b)

65 − 40 = 25

(c)

94 − 30 = 64

104

Exercises 22 and 23, pages 171-174

**5.** Subtract 14 from 56.

$$56 - 14 = \boxed{42}$$  56 − 10 − 4

**6.** Subtract 32 from 78.

$$78 - 32 = \boxed{46}$$

78 − 30 − 2

Exercise 24, pages 175-176

7. Subtract 3 from 49.

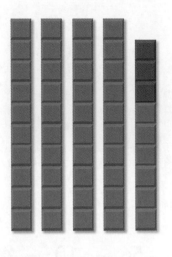

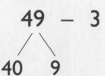

49 – 3

40    9

49 is 4 tens 9 ones.
Subtract 0 tens 3 ones.

First, subtract the ones.

```
Tens  Ones
  4    9
 −     3
 ─────────
       6
```

9 ones – 3 ones = 6 ones

Then, subtract the tens.

```
Tens  Ones
  4    9
 −     3
 ─────────
  4    6
```

4 tens – 0 tens = 4 tens

49 – 3 = 46

**8.** Subtract 6 from 57.

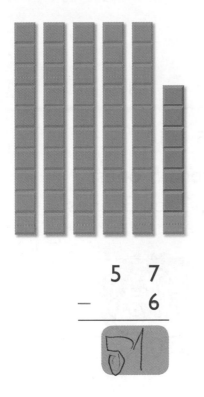

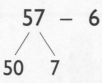

$$57 - 6$$

50   7

57 is 5 tens 7 ones.
Subtract 0 tens 6 ones.

```
    5   7
  -     6
  -------
     51
```

**9.** Subtract 5 from 69.

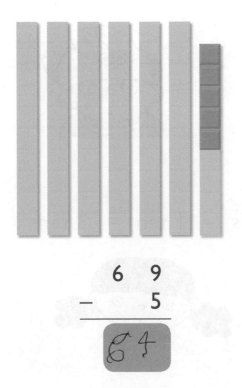

```
    6   9
  -     5
  -------
     64
```

10. Subtract 13 from 45.

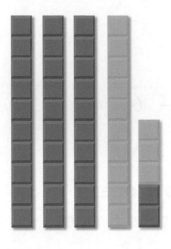

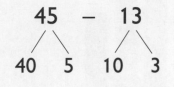

$$45 \quad - \quad 13$$

40   5    10   3

45 is 4 tens 5 ones.
Subtract 1 ten 3 ones.

First, subtract the ones.

| Tens | Ones |
|:---:|:---:|
| 4 | **5** |
| − 1 | **3** |
| | **2** |

5 ones − 3 ones = 2 ones

Then, subtract the tens.

| Tens | Ones |
|:---:|:---:|
| **4** | 5 |
| − **1** | 3 |
| **3** | **2** |

4 tens − 1 ten = 3 tens

45 − 13 = 32

11. Subtract 25 from 78.

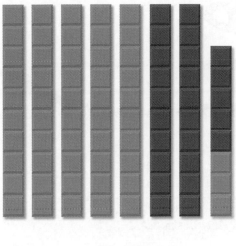

```
   7  8
-  2  5
─────────
```
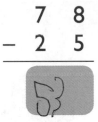

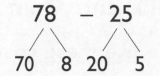

78 − 25

70  8  20  5

78 is 7 tens 8 ones.
Subtract 2 tens 5 ones.

12. Subtract 31 from 84.

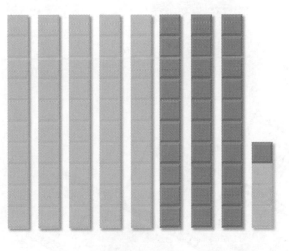

```
   8  4
-  3  1
─────────
```

Exercises 25, pages 177-180

Review 13, pages 181-185

**19**

# MONEY

## 1 Bills and Coins

We use these coins and bills in the U.S.

Do you know their values?

penny

nickel

dime

half dollar

quarter

one dollar

five dollars

ten dollars

twenty dollars

1.  Match the coins to the correct value.

The penny has the smallest value of all the coins.

Its value is 1 cent.

The nickel has a value of 5 cents.

The dime has a value of
10 cents.

The quarter has a value of
25 cents.

**2.**

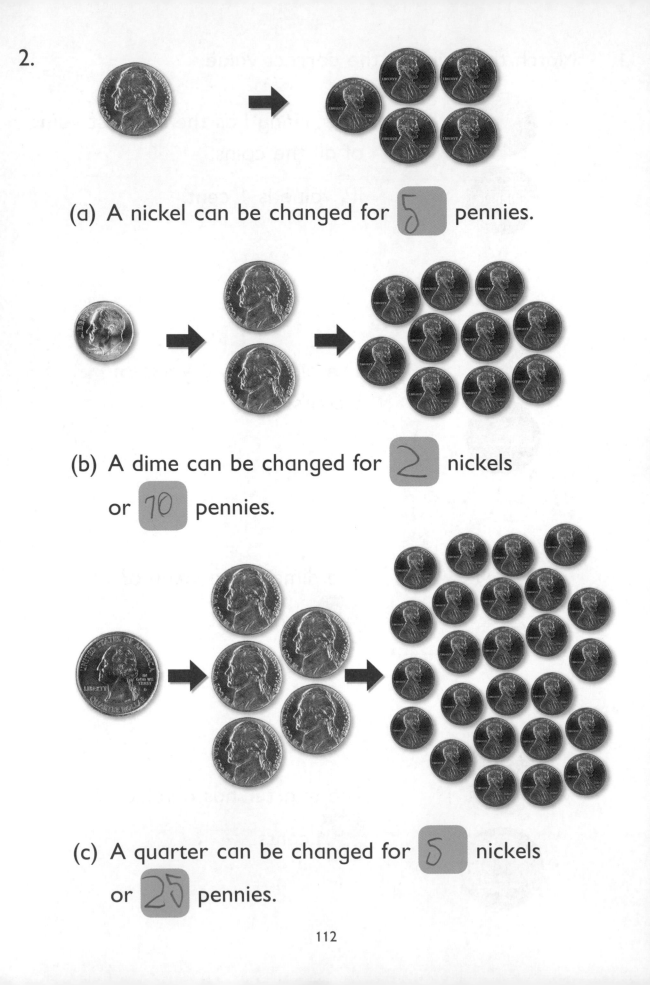

(a) A nickel can be changed for 5 pennies.

(b) A dime can be changed for 2 nickels

or 10 pennies.

(c) A quarter can be changed for 5 nickels

or 25 pennies.

**3.**

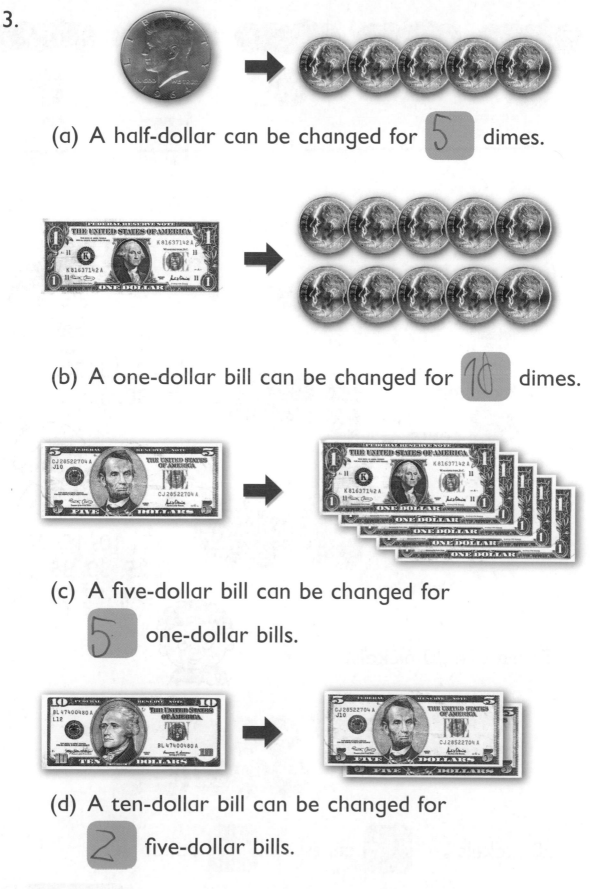

(a) A half-dollar can be changed for 5 dimes.

(b) A one-dollar bill can be changed for 10 dimes.

(c) A five-dollar bill can be changed for 5 one-dollar bills.

(d) A ten-dollar bill can be changed for 2 five-dollar bills.

**4.**

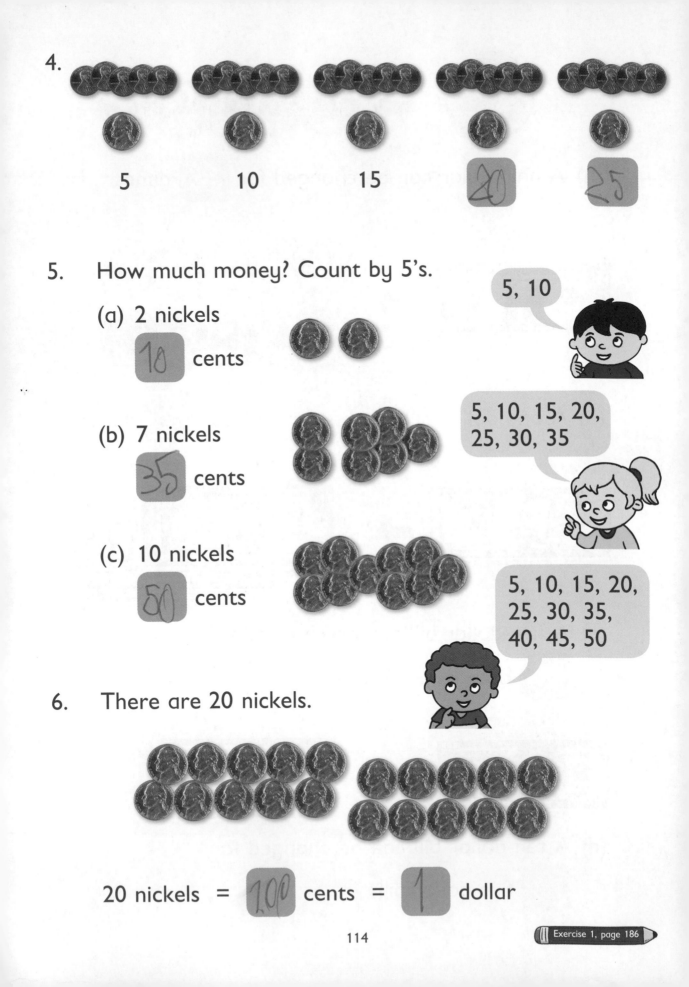

| 5 | 10 | 15 | 20 | 25 |

**5.** How much money? Count by 5's.

(a) 2 nickels

10 cents

5, 10

(b) 7 nickels

35 cents

5, 10, 15, 20,
25, 30, 35

(c) 10 nickels

50 cents

5, 10, 15, 20,
25, 30, 35,
40, 45, 50

**6.** There are 20 nickels.

20 nickels = 100 cents = 1 dollar

114

Exercise 1, page 186

7. Mary paid this amount of money for a notebook.

25, 50, 60, 70, 80, 90, 95 cents

The notebook cost 95 ¢.

8. Maria paid this amount of money for a doll.

10, 15, 16, 17 dollars

The doll cost $ 17 .

9. How much money is there in each set of coins?

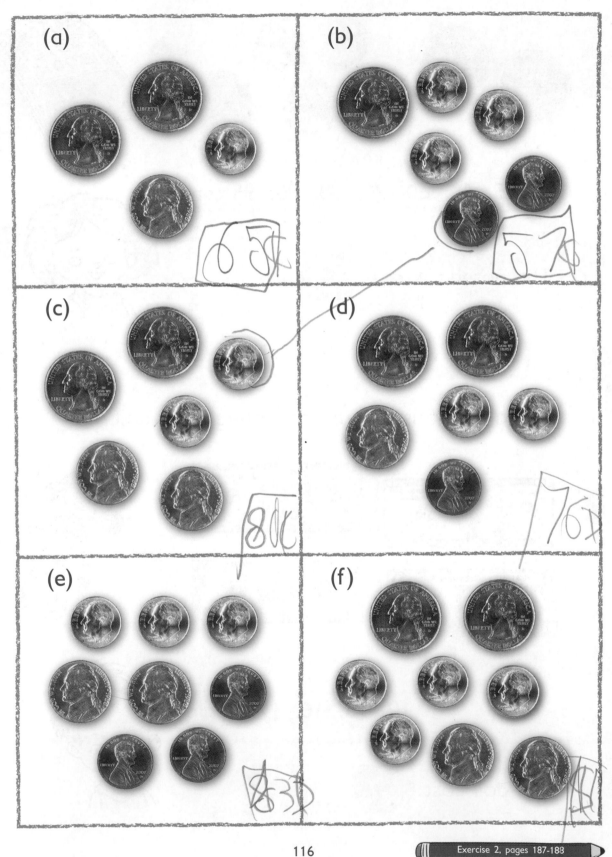

(a)

(b)

(c)

(d)

(e)

(f)

Exercise 2, pages 187-188

10. How much money is there in each set?

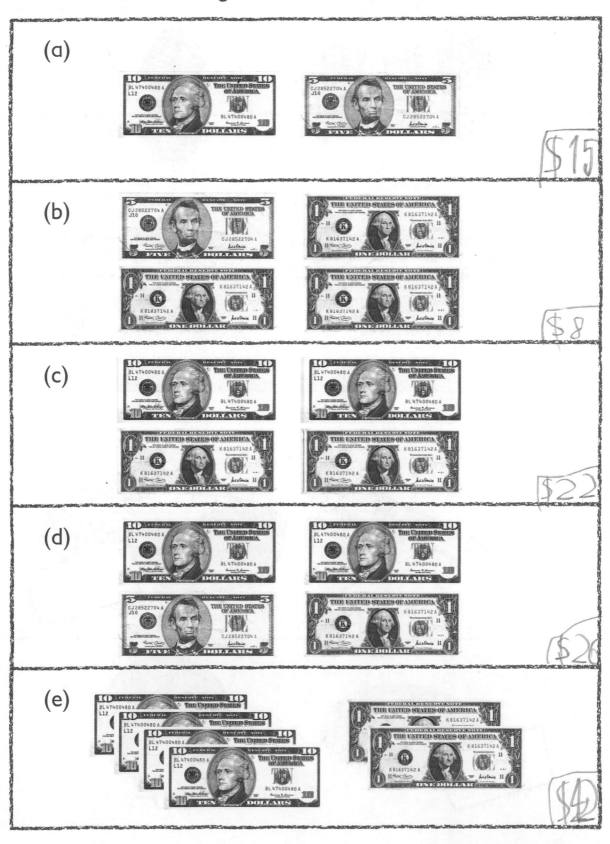

(a)

$15

(b)

$8

(c)

$22

(d)

$26

(e)

$42

Exercise 3, pages 189-190

11. Which set has a greater amount of money?

(a)

Set A                              Set B

(b)

Set X                              Set Y

12. Which is cheaper?

(a)

80¢                              95¢

(b)

$18                              $12

# ② Shopping

$17

45
−40
___
5

I have $20.
I have $3 left after
buying the doll.

Dani

$20 − $17 = $3

I have $15.
I do not have enough
money to buy the doll.
I need $2 more.

Emily

$17 − $15 = $2

**1.**

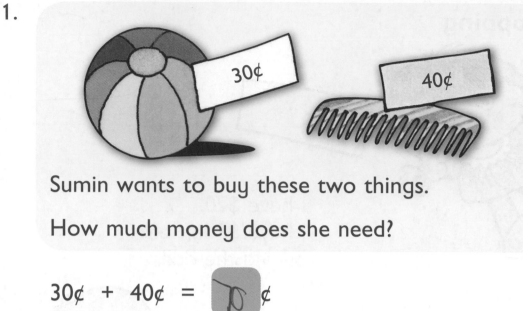

Sumin wants to buy these two things.

How much money does she need?

30¢ + 40¢ = 70 ¢

She needs 70¢.

**2.**

Mary has $9.

She wants to buy the purse.

How much more money does she need?

$12 − $9 = $3

She needs $3 more.

**3.**

Ali had $2 left after buying the bag.

How much did he have at first? 20

**4.**

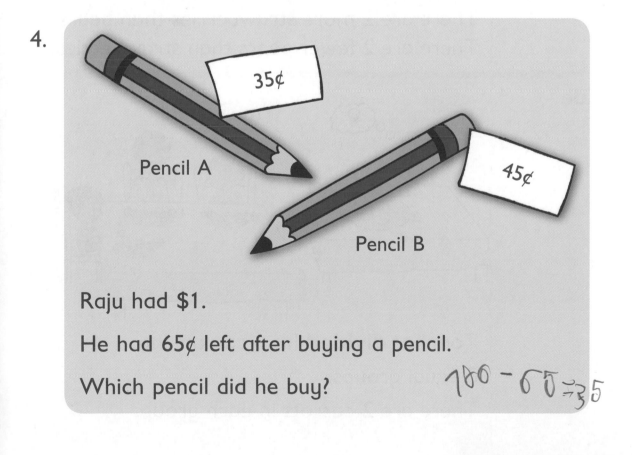

Pencil A 35¢

Pencil B 45¢

Raju had $1.

He had 65¢ left after buying a pencil.

Which pencil did he buy? 100 − 65 = 35

Exercise 5, pages 193-195

Reviews 14 and 15, pages 196-208

# GLOSSARY

| Word | Meaning |
|---|---|
| compare | When we **compare** numbers, we find out which number is greater or smaller. 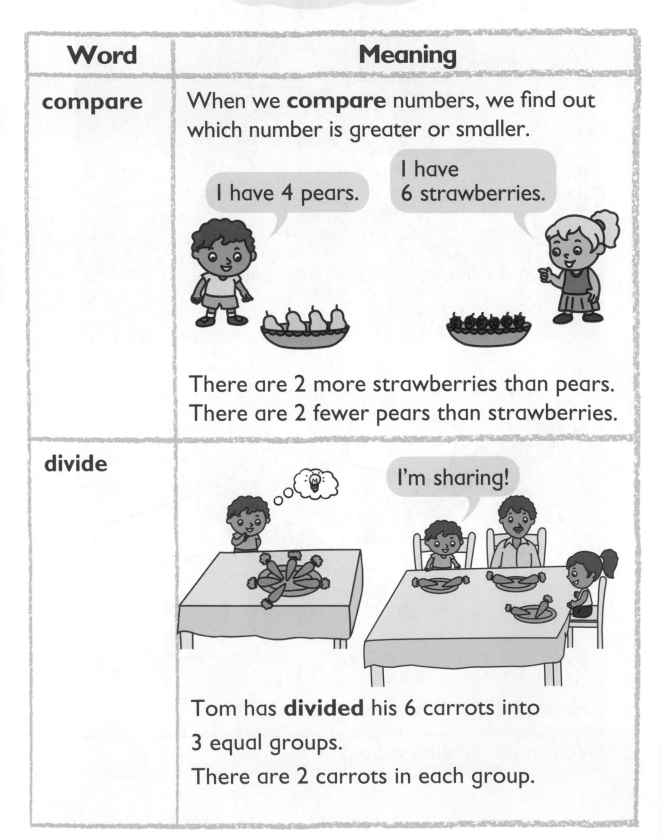 There are 2 more strawberries than pears. There are 2 fewer pears than strawberries. |
| divide | Tom has **divided** his 6 carrots into 3 equal groups. There are 2 carrots in each group. |

| Word | Meaning |
|---|---|
| **estimate** | We can **estimate** time. |
| | It is **about** 8 o'clock. |

It is a **little before**
8 o'clock.
It is **almost** 8 o'clock.

It is a **little after**
8 o'clock.

We can **estimate** numbers.

Bowl A            Bowl B

There are exactly 10 grapes in Bowl A.
There are **about** 20 grapes in Bowl B.

| **fourths** | |

halves            **fourths**

When we cut 1 whole into 4 equal parts,
we have 4 **fourths**.

| Word | Meaning |
|------|---------|
| **graph** | Graphs give us information. These are different kinds of **graphs**. |

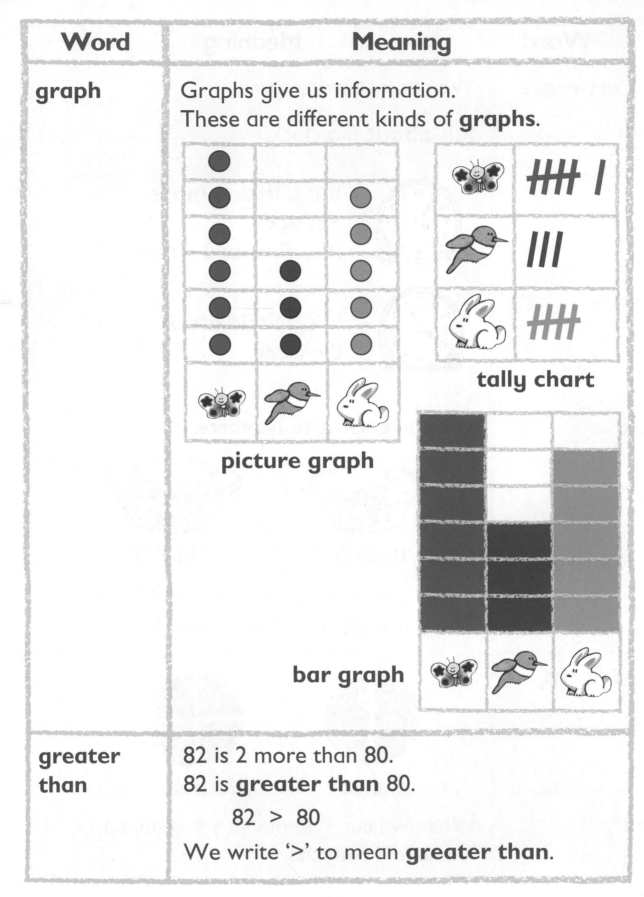

**picture graph**

**tally chart**

**bar graph**

| **greater than** | 82 is 2 more than 80. <br> 82 is **greater than** 80. <br><br>     82 > 80 <br><br> We write '>' to mean **greater than**. |
|------|---------|

| Word | Meaning |
|---|---|
| **group** | We put things in equal groups when we multiply or divide. <br><br> **3 groups** of 4 |
| **half past** | It is 30 minutes after 1 o'clock. <br> It is **half past** 1. |
| **halves** | whole      **halves** <br><br> When we cut 1 whole into 2 equal parts, we have 2 **halves**. |
| **less than** | 28 is **less than** 30. <br><br> 28 < 30 <br><br> We write '<' to mean **less than**. |

| Word | Meaning |
|------|---------|
| **multiply** | To put together equal groups. We write '×' to mean **multiply**.<br><br>$3 \times 2 = 6$<br><br>There are 3 equal groups.<br>There are 2 carrots in each group.<br>There are 6 carrots altogether. |
| **number pattern** | These are regular **number patterns**. We count on or backwards to find the pattern.<br><br>10 →(+10) 20 →(+10) 30 →(+10) 40 →(+10) 50<br><br>85 →(−2) 83 →(−2) 81 →(−2) 79 →(−2) 77 |
| **number sentence** | $3 + 3 = 6$      $6 - 3 = 3$<br>$3 \times 2 = 6$      $6 \div 2 = 3$<br><br>These are examples of **number sentences**. |
| **o'clock** | It is 1 **o'clock**. |

| Word | Meaning |
|------|---------|
| ones | 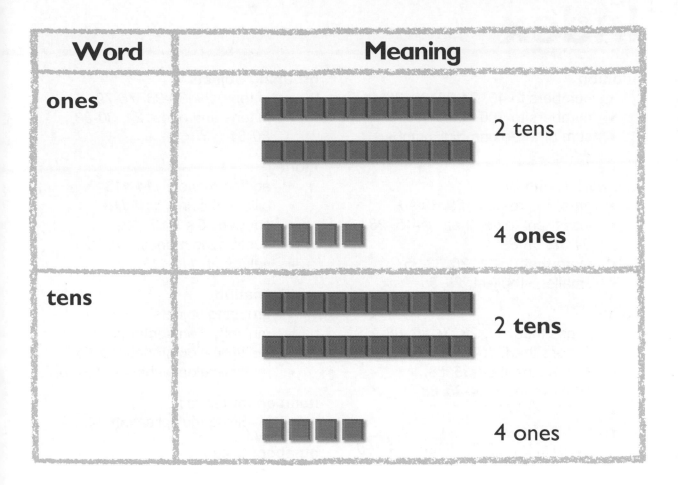 |
| tens | |

# Index